MW01073311

"...LOVE ONE ANOTHER..."
John 13:34

Basic Lesson Series—Volume 6

LOVE ONE ANOTHER

"Exercise thyself unto godliness"
1 Timothy 4:7

WATCHMAN NEE

Christian Fellowship Publishers, Inc.
New York

Copyright © 1975
Christian Fellowship Publishers, Inc.
New York
All Rights Reserved

ISBN 0-935008-10-1

Available from the Publishers at:

11515 Allecingie Parkway
Richmond, Virginia 23235

PRINTED IN U.S.A.

Basic Lessons—Volume 6

CONTENTS

BASIC LESSONS
ON
PRACTICAL CHRISTIAN LIVING

Burdened with the need of a firm foundation for the Christian life, brother Watchman Nee gave a series of basic lessons on practical Christian living during the training session for workers held in Kuling, Foochow, China in 1948. He expressed the hope that these essential lessons might be faithfully learned by God's people, thereby laying a good foundation for the building up of the Body of Christ.

These messages on practical Christian living have now been translated from the Chinese language and will be published in a series of six books, bearing the various titles of: (1) *A Living Sacrifice*; (2) *The Good Confession*; (3) *Assembling Together*; (4) *Not I, But Christ*; (5) *Do All to the Glory of God*; and (6) *Love One Another*.

"Exercise thyself unto godliness" (I Tim. 4:7), is the exhortation of the apostle Paul. May our hearts be so exercised by God's Word as to give the Holy Spirit opportunity to perfect the new creation.

All quotations of the Scriptures, unless otherwise indicated, are from the American Standard Version of the Bible (1901).

"... LOVE ONE ANOTHER ..."
John 13:34

GOVERNMENTAL FORGIVENESS

There are four kinds of forgiveness in the Bible. For convenience' sake, we shall give each a name: first, eternal forgiveness; second, borrowed forgiveness; third, communional forgiveness; and fourth, governmental forgiveness. In order to walk uprightly, we need to learn what God's governmental forgiveness is. Before we touch on this, however, let us first differentiate the four kinds of forgiveness.

Eternal Forgiveness

We call the forgiveness we receive at the time we are saved eternal forgiveness. This is the forgiveness of which the Lord Jesus spoke when He said, "Repentance and remission of sins should be preached in his name unto all the nations, beginning from Jerusalem" (Lk. 24:47). This is also what Romans 4:7 refers to: "Blessed are they whose iniquities are forgiven, and whose sins are covered."

We call this kind of forgiveness eternal forgiveness because once God forgives our sins, He forgives them forever. He casts our sins into the sea, into the depths of

1

the sea, so that He no longer sees nor remembers them. Such is the forgiveness we receive at the time of salvation. For us who believe in the Lord Jesus, He forgives all our sins and takes away all our iniquities so that before God none are left. This is eternal forgiveness.

Borrowed Forgiveness

Many times God Himself says, "I forgive you!" Sometimes, though, He declares His forgiveness through the church: "God has forgiven your sins!" This kind of forgiveness we term borrowed forgiveness. "And when he had said this, he breathed on them, and saith unto them, Receive ye the Holy Spirit: whose soever sins ye forgive, they are forgiven unto them; whose soever sins ye retain, they are retained" (John 20:22–23). Here the Lord gives His Holy Spirit to the church so that she may represent Him on earth and be His vessel to forgive people's sins. Though we call this borrowed forgiveness, we need to exercise extreme care lest we fall into the error of the Roman Catholic church. Notice what the Lord said. The forgiveness here is based on the Lord's breathing upon the church, saying, "Receive ye the Holy Spirit." The consequence of receiving the Holy Spirit is that the church knows whose sins are retained and whose are forgiven. Thus the church may declare whose sins are retained and whose sins are forgiven. Remember this: the church has such authority only because she herself is under the authority of the Holy Spirit. "Whose soever sins ye forgive, they are forgiven unto them; whose soever sins ye retain, they are retained"—these words come after "Receive ye the Holy Spirit." Borrowed forgiveness is God forgiving people's sins through the channel of the church.

Sometimes we meet a sinner who feels guilty after hearing the gospel. We bring him to God and he confesses that he is a sinner. He asks God to forgive his sins. He cries, he sheds tears, he repents and honestly receives the Lord Jesus. But, being a heathen, he knows nothing of the truth of salvation. If, at this moment, there is someone who can represent the church and declare to him, "God has forgiven your sins!", this would be an excellent thing to do, for it would spare him much sorrow and many doubts. Whenever you see a person who has truly believed, you can tell him, "Today you have received the Lord; now you may thank God, for He has already forgiven your sins." If the church cannot forgive or retain sins, how can she decide who may be baptized and who may not? Why do you baptize some people and refuse to baptize others? Why do you receive some to the breaking of bread and refuse others? These are instances in which the church exercises the authority the Lord has given her to declare who is saved and who is not saved, whose sins are forgiven and whose sins are retained. Such words may not be idly spoken but only under the authority of the Holy Spirit. The church, having received the Holy Spirit, is under His authority, and is thus like a borrowed hand to God. The Lord borrows the hand of the church to declare whose sins are forgiven and whose sins are retained. This, then, is the second kind of forgiveness in the Bible: instead of forgiving sins directly, God uses the hand of the church to forgive people's sins. In eternal forgiveness, God directly forgives sins, but in borrowed forgiveness, God announces His forgiveness by man's hand.

3

Communional Forgiveness

What is communional forgiveness? "But if we walk in the light, as he is in the light, we have fellowship one with another, and the blood of Jesus his Son cleanseth us from all sin. If we say that we have no sin, we deceive ourselves, and the truth is not in us. If we confess our sins, he is faithful and righteous to forgive us our sins, and to cleanse us from all unrighteousness" (1 John 1:7-9). "My little children, these things write I unto you that ye may not sin. And if any man sin, we have an Advocate with the Father, Jesus Christ the righteous: and he is the propitiation for our sins; and not for ours only, but also for the whole world" (2:1-2). The forgiveness mentioned here is neither that which we received at the time of salvation nor that which the church extends to us. After we believe in the Lord and become God's children, we still may have need of God's forgiveness. We have mentioned this before as the forgiveness of the red heifer.* Though we have received eternal forgiveness, we may weaken and once again sin before the Lord, thus interrupting our fellowship with God. So, once again we need forgiveness.

Life has a special characteristic—it delights in fellowship. Or, as biology students know, we may say that life has two basic features: self-preservation—to keep oneself alive and away from death, for life fears to die; and fellowship—the fear of being isolated. If you put a chicken alone in one place, it will show boredom; but if you put many chickens together, they will manifest great liveliness. A man imprisoned in solitary confinement suffers greatly because of being unable to communicate with other people. Man, like other living creatures, desires to preserve his own life as well as to have fellowship with others.

* Volume 4, *Not I But Christ*, Lesson 22

For you who have trusted in the blood of the Lord Jesus, the life preservation problem is already solved. You have no more trouble because you are eternally saved and your sins are eternally forgiven.

But there may be trouble in another respect. If you sin against God after you are saved, your fellowship with God as well as with God's children may be disturbed. What does this mean? Let us use an example: after her mother has gone out, a girl steals into the kitchen and, without permission, eats some goodies. When she is finished eating, she wipes her mouth clean, cleans off the table, and closes the kitchen door. But she has already committed a sin! Usually she and her mother have very intimate fellowship in the evenings, but tonight it cannot be the same. When her mother calls her from upstairs, her heart jumps downstairs! She thinks that her mother is going to beat her. Even when her mother gives supper to her, she cannot enjoy the food. She is afraid that her mother has discovered what she did. All evening she tries to evade her mother. As you can see, her fellowship with her mother is disturbed. Of course, just because she has stolen some food does not mean that she is no longer a daughter. No, she is still a daughter, but the fellowship with her mother has been disturbed. Likewise, not because you have sinned have you ceased to be God's child; you are still His child, though your sin has caused your fellowship with Him to be immediately interrupted. No longer is your conscience without offense, and, to enjoy uninterrupted fellowship with God, you must have a clear conscience. When one's conscience is offended, fellowship with God becomes impossible.

God's children will not lose their position as His children because of sin, but they will certainly lose their fellowship with Him. Therefore, God has provided a kind of forgiveness which we call communional forgiveness. Why do we call it communional forgiveness? Because by coming to God and confessing your sin, you may have your communion and fellowship with God restored. Otherwise you have no way of having your fellowship restored. You cannot pray, you cannot even say "Amen" to another's prayer. What then can you do? What should the girl in our parable do? She must come to her mother and confess that she has stolen food which she should not have. She needs to learn to stand on her mother's side of the matter and say that she has sinned. She must call sin by its proper name and say, "Please forgive my sin!" In like manner, we must come to God and confess that we have sinned against Him in a certain matter and ask His forgiveness. "If we confess our sins, He is faithful and righteous to forgive us our sins and to cleanse us from all unrighteousness." Such forgiveness is not connected to eternal salvation but is related to fellowship with God. Therefore, we call it communional forgiveness.

Governmental Forgiveness

There is still another kind of forgiveness which we call governmental forgiveness. This kind of forgiveness is seen in the following Bible passages: Matt. 9:2, 5–6; James 5:15 and Matt. 6:14–15, 18, 21–35.

What is God's governmental forgiveness? I am convinced that if I had known the government of God immediately following my salvation, I would have been spared many troubles and problems.

The parable of the girl may be continued here: formerly

6

the mother always left the doors in the house open, including the cupboard door and the kitchen door. She never locked the cupboard in which she put food. But this time, when she came home, she discovered that some of the food in the cupboard had been eaten. Now that the mother knows what has happened, the girl is forced to confess her sin and ask for forgiveness. The mother forgives her and even kisses her. The incident is considered past and the fellowship is restored. However, next time the mother leaves the house, she locks all the doors. Her way of doing things has changed. Fellowship is one thing, but government is quite another.

What is government? Government is a way. God's government is God's way, God's administration. The mother may forgive the girl's sin and restore their fellowship, but next time she will lock both the cupboard and the kitchen doors when she goes out. In other words, she has changed her way. To restore fellowship is easy, but to restore the way is not so easy. The mother is afraid that her daughter may do it again. She cannot give the daughter full liberty but has to put on some restraints. Her way has changed. Remember, God treats us in a similar manner. Communional forgiveness is relatively easy to get. He who sincerely confesses his sin will have his fellowship restored. At the moment he confesses his sin, God restores fellowship with him. Nevertheless, God may change His way toward him. It may be that God's discipline will immediately come upon him; God may not give him as much liberty as he enjoyed before.

Again, another day may come when God removes His disciplinary hand—and this we call governmental forgiveness. In the case of the mother, this would mean that the day comes when she feels her daughter is now dependable, so she leaves the doors unlocked. This is governmental forgiveness.

Communional forgiveness is one thing, governmental forgiveness is quite another. Another example of this would be a father who has several sons. He lets his sons go out to play in the afternoons from four o'clock till six o'clock, the time for supper. One day they go out and fight with other children. The father forgives them and still allows them to go out. But what would happen if these children fight every day when they go out? What would the father do then? Though the children might confess their sin daily and daily get forgiveness, yet the father would feel that his way must be wrong, that his government of his children must not be right. So he tells his sons, "Because you fight every day you go out, starting tomorrow, you will be shut in the house." This is the father's hand.

You, too, may sin against God, and at each confession of your sin God forgives you. This does not, however, hinder God from giving you new chastening. Since God has forgiven you, your fellowship with God may be restored. But God will change His way with you. It is important for us to know that God's disciplinary hand upon us is not easily moved, nor, once extended, is it easily removed. Unless God has full assurance that His children are all right, His governmental hand will not be removed. To go back to our second parable: Seeing his sons getting into fights every day, the father shuts them inside for a week, two weeks, a month, or even two months until he is satisfied that his sons will not be mischievous and fight with others. Then perhaps he will tell his sons that since they have been fairly good during these two months, they will be allowed to go out the next day for ten minutes. The father begins to remove his governmental hand. Those ten minutes outside we may call governmental forgiveness. The government starts to change, though the father still watches how his sons conduct themselves with other children. If they do not fight during those ten minutes, he may give them half an hour outside the second day. Later on, he may allow them to play for an hour. After one or two months, he may permit them to play outside from four o'clock to six o'clock as they used to do. When that day arrives, his governmental forgiveness is fully granted his sons.

Therefore, brethren, what is governmental forgiveness? It is something quite different from eternal forgiveness, borrowed forgiveness, or communional forgiveness. It is something which speaks of God's taking care of us, dealing with us, and disciplining us.

1. THE MEANING OF GOD'S GOVERNMENTAL HAND

There are many passages in the Bible which are related to this. For instance, "Whatsoever a man soweth, that shall he also reap" (Gal. 6:7). This is God's governmental hand. Suppose a father is always lenient with his children. Naturally his children will be wild and undisciplined. How can the house be in order if the father never rules the house? If a man often quarrels with people, the natural consequence will be that he is without any friends. You see, whatsoever a man sows, that shall he also reap. This is God's government, His appointed hand, and it cannot be changed. Be very careful, children of God, lest you stir up God's governmental hand; for, once stirred, it is hard to be removed.

The Story of the Palsied

Some people brought a man sick of the palsy to the Lord. The scribes were present at the time. "Son, . . . thy sins are forgiven!" said the Lord Jesus to the palsied. These words of the Lord's constitute a real problem to those who do not know what governmental forgiveness is. This palsied man was brought to the Lord by his friends; he himself never expressed faith in the Lord. Yet, the Lord said to him, "Son, thy sins are forgiven!" Does this mean that as soon as the palsied man was brought to the Lord his soul was saved? If this were the case, salvation would be very easy to get, for, just by being brought to the Lord, one's sins would be immediately forgiven. No, the forgiveness here is definitely not eternal forgiveness; neither does it have any relationship to borrowed forgiveness nor to communional forgiveness. It is another kind of forgiveness, since the Lord shows us two things here: on the one side, "Thy sins are forgiven"; on the other side, "Arise and walk." Let us remember that many sicknesses are due to God's governmental hand. In order to heal the palsied man and get him to walk, the Lord has to first grant him governmental forgiveness. The forgiveness seen here was related to God's government. It had a special connection with sickness. Hence, when the palsied man was brought to the Lord Jesus for healing, the Lord said nothing but "Thy sins are forgiven." In other words, with the forgiveness of sins, the sickness would be healed. His sickness was connected to his sins. The Lord Jesus so spoke because He knew the cause of the palsy was the man's sins before God. When his sins were forgiven, his sickness was over. This we call governmental forgiveness. When governmental forgiveness comes, sickness is healed. It is evident that this man had sinned against God's government and therefore had gotten the palsy. Having been forgiven of his sins by the Lord, he could arise, take up his bedding, and return home. So the forgiveness here is different from the other kinds of forgiveness. This kind is governmental forgiveness.

The Elders Pray and Anoint

"Is any among you sick? Let him call for the elders of the church; and let them pray over him, anointing him with oil in the name of the Lord: and the prayer of faith shall save him that is sick, and the Lord shall raise him up; and if he have committed sins, it shall be forgiven him" (Jas. 5:14-15). The forgiveness here seems to be very special. We have seen before that there are many causes for sickness.* Not all sickness is caused by sin, but some sickness is. The sins here are forgiven, not through the confession of the sick, but by the prayer of the elders of the church. What is this? Surely this forgiveness is not eternal forgiveness, nor borrowed forgiveness, nor communional forgiveness. Probably this forgiveness is also related to governmental forgiveness. Let us, by way of an example, assume that a brother is sick because of having fallen into the governmental hand of God. He is chastened by God because he has sinned and fallen. When he confesses his sin before God, he receives forgiveness and his fellowship with God is restored. But the disciplinary hand of God still has not left him. It awaits the day when the elders of the church come and pray for him, telling him that the brethren have also forgiven him and are eager for him to

* Watchman Nee, *The Spiritual Man.* 3 vols. New York, Christian Fellowship Publishers, 1968. Translated from the Chinese. See the chapter entitled "Sickness" in vol. 3, especially pp. 179-195.—*Translator*

11

be revived, that the church is anxious to see him restored to the flow of life. When that day comes, the elders anoint him with oil that the anointing oil of the Head may flow to him. As the church prays for him, the brother is restored. When the governmental hand of God is thus removed from him, his sickness may be healed. This is what is meant by, "If he have committed sins, it shall be forgiven him." The sins referred to here are not ordinary sins, but those which bring God's governmental hand. In reading the Bible, we need to understand that James 5 speaks of God's governmental hand. If you fall into God's governmental hand, He will not let you go until you get forgiveness.

The Story of David

In order to understand the meaning of governmental forgiveness, we will use David as an illustration. Nowhere in the whole Bible is God's governmental forgiveness so clearly presented as in the case of David and the wife of Uriah. David committed two sins: he committed adultery and he committed murder. In adultery, he sinned against the wife of Uriah; in murder, he sinned against Uriah. After he had committed these two sins, he confessed them to God. This is shown in Psalm 51 and other psalms. Deeply contrite in heart, he honestly confessed his sins before God. He acknowledged that what he had done was ugly, unclean, and offensive. It is clear that after David confessed his sins in Psalm 51, his fellowship with God was restored. This is like the first chapter of 1 John.

Yet what did God say to David when He sent Nathan to him? Notice Nathan's words: "And David said unto Nathan, I have sinned against Jehovah. And Nathan said unto David, Jehovah also hath put away thy sin; thou shalt not die" (2 Sam. 12:13). David said, "I have sinned against Jehovah." He confessed his sins and acknowledged his uncleanness. So God sent Nathan to tell him that the Lord had put away his sin, that therefore he would not die. This clearly indicates that David's sin has been forgiven. But God had more to say to David. First, "Howbeit, because by this deed thou has given great occasion to the enemies of Jehovah to blaspheme, the child also that is born unto thee shall surely die" (v. 14). Second, "Now therefore the sword shall never depart from thy house, because thou hast despised me, and hast taken the wife of Uriah the Hittite to be thy wife" (v. 10). Third, "Thus saith Jehovah, Behold, I will raise up evil against thee out of thine own house; and I will take thy wives before thine eyes, and give them unto thy neighbor, and he shall lie with thy wives in the sight of this sun. For thou didst it secretly: but I will do this thing before all Israel, and before the sun" (vv. 11–12). Though God had put away David's sin, yet He caused his son born of the wife of Uriah to die. And again, though God had put away David's sin, He nevertheless bade the sword never depart from David's house. And once more, though God had certainly put away David's sin, He still permitted Absalom to rebel against David and defile David's wives. In other words, though David's sin was forgiven, the chastening did not immediately depart from him.

Let me speak very frankly. Whatever sin you may have committed, if you go to God and ask for forgiveness, you will be forgiven. The restoration of fellowship can be very fast. David could quickly restore his fellowship with God. Nevertheless, the discipline of God upon David stayed until even after his death. With God's discipline upon him,

13

God's government did not depart. Therefore, it followed that his son got sick. Though David fasted and lay on the ground, it was all to no avail. The disciplinary hand of God had fallen upon David. The son finally died. Later on, other things happened: David's firstborn son, Amnon, was murdered and, after that, another son, Absalom, rebelled. The sword never departed from David's house. Nonetheless, God told David that He had forgiven his sins. Brethren, God is willing to forgive all the sins that you commit, but that does not mean that you can prevent Him from disciplining you or letting His governmental hand fall upon you.

2. HUMBLE YOURSELF UNDER GOD'S MIGHTY HAND

Our God is the God of government. Sometimes when He is offended, He does not immediately move His governmental hand. He just lets you get by. But once He moves His governmental hand, there is nothing you can do except to humble yourself. There is no way for you to escape; He is not like man who will easily allow you to get away. To have your sin forgiven and your fellowship with God restored is quite easy. But you cannot remove the discipline God gives you in your environment—your home, your business, or your physical body. The only thing you can do is learn to subject yourself to the mighty hand of God. The humbler we are under His mighty hand and the less we resist, the easier it will be to have the governmental hand of God removed from us. If we are not submissive and patient, if we murmur and fret within, let me tell you, it will be harder for God's governmental hand to be removed. This is a most serious matter. Twenty years ago you did something according to your own idea. Today you meet the same thing again and you have yet to eat that fruit of your earlier action. That thing has come back and found you out. What should you do when this happens? You should bow your head, saying: "Lord, it is my fault!" You should humble yourself under God's hand and not resist. The more you resist, the heavier the hand of God. So I always say that you must subject yourself to the mighty hand of God. The more you resist God's governmental hand, the more things will happen to you. As soon as the governmental hand of God is upon you, you must humble yourself and gladly acknowledge that you deserve it, for the Lord cannot be wrong. You should be in subjection. You must not think of rebelling; you must not even murmur or fret.

If you are insubordinate and think of escaping from God's hand, remember, it is not an easy thing to do. Who can escape God's hand? Do you not realize that it is what you did before that has caused you to fall into today's situation? For example: In his childhood a brother liked to eat candy. He ate so much candy that his teeth suffered much decay. One day he became conscious of his indulgence and its effect. He asked God to forgive him the sin of indulging himself too much in candy. He easily got forgiveness from God for this sin, but this did not stop his teeth from decaying. God's government was upon him. Too much candy causes tooth decay. If you confess your sin, your fellowship may be restored but that will not cause you to grow good teeth. It is God's government and you should learn to submit yourself to it. (Naturally, decayed teeth will not be restored. However, there are certain things which, after God's governmental hand has been removed, may be restored.)

Let me use another illustration from the Bible: After the incident of striking the rock at Meribah (Num. 20:10–12),

15

Moses and Aaron fell into the governmental hand of God. Though Aaron failed, God still permitted him to be priest and to have his fellowship restored. Later on, however, God told him that he must depart from this world and not enter the land of Canaan. Moses, too, did not sanctify Jehovah at the rock. Instead of speaking to the rock as God commanded, Moses smote it with the rod. Because of this, God's hand came upon him and he too was unable to enter Canaan. Do you see the basic principle? It is God's government. You can no longer hold God to the way in which He formerly treated you. You may have to change your way hereafter. You may even have to change from the way which you think best.

The Bible is full of such instances. When the people of Israel came to Kadesh in the wilderness of Paran, they sent spies to spy out the land (see Num. 13 and 14). The spies cut down a branch with a cluster of grapes so big it needed two men to carry it. They knew the land was indeed flowing with milk and honey. But they were afraid and refused to enter into the land because they saw that the people there were of such great stature that the Israelites were in their own sight as grasshoppers. As a result, except for Joshua and Caleb who later entered into the land, all the rest of the people were to die in the wilderness. When they heard God pronounce this judgment, they confessed their sin and expressed their readiness to enter in. Though God did indeed continue to treat them with grace and acknowledge them as His people, He did not allow them to have any part in Canaan. They were not allowed to enter in, for the government of God had changed. Therefore, brethren, from the beginning of your Christian life you should desire to walk from that day to the last day on the road which God has arranged for you. Do not live loosely; do not sin! Please remember: though you may still receive mercy, yet you may find that God has had to change His way for you. His governmental hand never relaxes.

God's governmental hand is truly most serious. Let us be fearful, for we do not know when the disciplinary hand of God will come upon us. God may allow some to get by all the time. Or He may overlook rebellion ten times but on the eleventh time bring His hand down. Or His hand may come down the very first time. We have no way of knowing when His disciplinary hand will descend. God's government is not something we can control. Whatever He wishes, He does.

Because of this, brethren, we must first of all try our very best to learn to be obedient to the Lord. May God be merciful and gracious to you that you may not fall into the governmental hand of God. Howbeit, if you do fall into His governmental hand, do not resist or be rash. Do not attempt to run away, but hold on to the basic principle of subjection at any cost. You cannot naturally by yourself be submissive, but you can ask the Lord to make you so. Only by the mercy of the Lord can you get through. "O Lord, be merciful to me that I may get through!" If God's governmental hand has not fallen upon you, look persistently for His mercy. If it has already fallen, if He has allowed you to be sick or to have difficulties come upon you, remember well that you should never by your fleshly hand try to resist God's government. As soon as God's government falls on you, humble yourself at once under His mighty hand. You should say, "Lord, this is Your doing, this is Your arrangement; I gladly submit, I am willing to accept it." When God's governmental hand fell on Job (it could have been avoided), the more submissive

17

Job was, the better his condition was; the more he boasted of his own righteousness, the worse his situation became.

Thank God, frequently God's governmental hand does not stay forever on a person. I personally believe that when God's governmental hand does fall on a person, sometimes the prayer of the church may easily remove that hand. This is what is so precious in James 5. There James tells us that the elders of the church may remove the governmental hand of God. He says: "And the prayer of faith shall save him that is sick, and the Lord shall raise him up; and if he have committed sins, it shall be forgiven him." So, when a brother finds that this is the way for him, the church may pray for him and help to remove God's governmental hand from him.

I remember once hearing Miss Margaret E. Barber say a most wonderful thing. A brother who had done something wrong and later repented came to see her. This was what she said to him: "Is it not that you have now repented and come back? You should go to God and say to Him, 'I was originally a vessel in the potter's hand, but now this vessel has been broken.' You should not force the Lord by saying, 'Lord, you must make me the same vessel.' No, you should humbly pray, 'Lord, be merciful to me and again make me a vessel. I dare not force your hand. It is fine with me, Lord, whether you make me a noble vessel or an ignoble vessel!' "

People think that since they will always be the same vessel, they would like the Lord to make them more glorious, more noble. Sometimes people even ask the Lord to make them into a better vessel. There are times when we even manage to get blessing out of curse. But there is one thing I wish to tell you: those of us who have had many dealings with the Lord know that we often fall into

18

God's hand, into His governmental hand. We acknowledge that through that governmental hand God teaches us what His will is. All we can do is submit. There is no way to escape; just submit.

We should not take these things lightly. A certain sister consulted with me when she was thinking of marrying. I told her that so far as I could see she should not marry that man because he did not seem to be a dependable Christian. She insisted, though, that she had confidence in him. So she married him. After eight months, she wrote me a long letter in which she said, "I know I was wrong. I did not listen to you, and now I know I have committed a great error. What should I do now?" My reply to her was: "Hereafter you have only one way, and that is, humble yourself under the mighty hand of God. If you should write me the second time, I still cannot help you. Nobody can help you, for you have fallen into the governmental hand of God. When you are in God's governmental hand, do not try to struggle against it. If you do, you will be a broken vessel and there will be no future for you." In that letter, I also emphatically told her that it would be wrong for her to write me again. So, let us remember: nothing can be more serious than the government of God.

I often think about the condition of the church today. It is like going to a potter's house and finding in the field there many broken bowls, broken basins, and broken flasks—all broken vessels. Such is the condition of Christians today. It is indeed a most serious thing. I repeat, we must learn to submit ourselves to God's mighty hand.

3. Be a God-Fearing Person

There are two passages in the Bible which also speak of God's governmental hand. These are Matthew 6:15 and

18:23–25. One thing of special importance is that we should not carelessly judge others. This is most serious, for in whatever matter you carelessly judge others, that same thing may easily fall upon you. In whatever thing you do not forgive others, that is what may come upon you. This again shows the governmental hand of God. If you do not forgive another's debt, God will not forgive your sin. This is governmental forgiveness, something altogether different from eternal forgiveness. Yes, God *is* your heavenly Father; the question of eternity is already settled. But if a brother should sin against you and you will not forgive him, God also will not forgive you. His governmental hand will fall on you. Therefore, let me tell you: learn to be generous and forgiving; be charitable, be ready to forgive others. If you are always complaining and criticizing others and finding fault with their conduct, you may fall into God's government. It will not be easy for you to extricate yourself, for God will certainly dig deep in you. If you are tight with others, God will be tight with you. Remember the servant in Matthew 18 who emerged from his master's house and found his fellow-servant who owed him a hundred shillings. He took him by the throat and demanded payment. When the master heard the news, he was greatly displeased. He ordered that servant to be delivered to the tormentors till he should pay all that was due. God began to chasten him and with the governmental hand of God upon him, he could not easily get away.

Consequently, we must not only learn to be charitable in the matter of forgiving but also we must be careful not to freely speak and criticize others. Oftentimes that which we speak against and criticize in others will soon be seen in us. Frequently we have observed how quickly discipline has come upon one who is too severe toward others. If you judge the head of a family who has problems with his children by saying, "Behold, the hand of God is always upon him," it may not take long for the same trouble to descend on you. Brethren, let us learn to be afraid of God's government. Let us learn to fear God.

May I say this to you: it takes a lifetime to learn the government of God. All our years on earth as Christians are spent learning to know how God rules over us. Remember, in nothing can we freely judge or criticize. Let us develop the habit of not being busybodies or babblers. Learn to be God-fearing. It is not only unprofitable, but also most serious to provoke the governmental hand of God. Be very careful not to let the predicament of others fall upon you; do not draw it down upon yourself by freely condemning others. Whatever we sow, that we shall also reap. This maxim is very true for God's children. Let us learn to be charitable. The more charitable we are the better, for by being charitable toward other people, we will receive charity from God. If we are mean and severe with our brothers, God will be strict and exacting with us. Learn to be gentle, merciful, and kind toward the brethren. Try to overlook the faults of your brethren; speak fewer idle words, be restrained in judgment. When people are in trouble, help them but do not judge them.

In the last days the Jews are going to suffer much. They will be imprisoned, stripped naked, and left hungry. Those who are sheep (see Matt. 25:31–46) will visit them in prison, clothe them in their nakedness, and feed them in their hunger. We cannot say that because God has decided to let the Jews pass through persecution and distress, we then will add to their sufferings. Yes, God does allow them to pass through deep waters, but we must learn to be charitable. Governmental discipline is God's province; the concern of the children of God in this age is to learn to be charitable and merciful to others no matter what the circumstances. Thus shall God spare us many distresses.

There are many Christians who have fallen terribly because of judging people too severely in the past. Their difficulty issues out of their past criticism. God has not lessened His rein. Let us therefore be charitable toward people lest we fall into the governmental hand of God. Learn to love people and treat them generously. May God be merciful to us for our follies in conduct and in deed that we may not come under His governmental hand. In this respect, we are cast on God's mercy. How much we need to live by God's wisdom. Let us tell God that we are but fools and often act so foolishly, that if we fall into His governmental hand we will easily be cracked. Let us ask Him for mercy. Let me tell you: the more humble and tender you are, the more easily you will come out from under God's government. The more proud and self-justifying you are, the harder it will be for you to get out from under it. So, learn to be humble.

In case we do fall into God's governmental hand, whether for something large or something small, we must never rebel. Rebelliousness is downright foolishness. The one and only principle we can follow is to humble ourselves under the mighty hand of God. If we really humble ourselves, we will see that "in due time" God will let us go free. Then He will consider the matter closed. I hope you will notice especially these words, "in due time": "Humble yourselves therefore under the mighty hand of God, that he may exalt you in due time" (1 Pet. 5:6). The emphasis here is "in due time." In due time, God will open the way out for you; in due time, He will give you a straight path; in due time, He will set you free; and in due time, He will exalt you.

"Under the mighty hand of God" here points exclusively to His discipline; hence we must humble ourselves under that hand. There is no meaning of protection in the phrase, for if protection were meant, it would speak of His everlasting arm. To humble ourselves under His mighty hand simply means to submit. This is the mighty hand which you can neither move nor resist. Say to the Lord, "Lord, I am willing to listen. Whatever place You may put me in, I gladly accept. I will not resist. I have no opinion about the way You have treated me. I gladly hear Your word. I am ready to stay in the situation as long as You wish." Then you will see that "in due time" He will release you. No one knows how long this will take. When the time comes that the Lord thinks you have learned your lesson, He may move the church to pray for your release.

It is my desire that brothers and sisters would know the government of God from the very beginning of their Christian life. Many of our difficulties are caused by the lack of this knowledge. I hope that from the very first day of the first year God's children will know God's government. This will help them to walk ahead in a straight path.

THE DISCIPLINE OF GOD

Ye have not yet resisted unto blood, striving against sin: and ye have forgotten the exhortation which reasoneth with you as with sons,

> My son, regard not lightly the chastening
> of the Lord,
> Nor faint when thou art reproved of him;
> For whom the Lord loveth he chasteneth,
> And scourgeth every son whom he receiveth.

It is for chastening that ye endure; God dealeth with you as with sons; for what son is there whom his father chasteneth not? But if ye are without chastening, whereof all have been made partakers, then are ye bastards, and not sons. Furthermore, we had the fathers of our flesh to chasten us, and we gave them reverence: shall we not much rather be in subjection unto the Father of spirits, and live? For they indeed for a few days chastened us as seemed good to them; but he for our profit, that we may be partakers of his holiness. All chastening seemeth for the present to be not joyous but grievous; yet afterward it yieldeth peaceable fruit unto them that have been exercised thereby, even the fruit of righteousness. Wherefore lift up the hands that hang down, and the palsied knees; and make straight paths for your feet, that that which is lame be not turned out of the way, but rather be healed.

Hebrews 12:4–13

The Meaning of Discipline

"Ye have not yet resisted unto blood, striving against sin" (12:4). The apostle told the Hebrews that, though in their striving against sin they had suffered much and met with many trials and persecutions, they had not yet resisted unto blood. In this respect they fell short of what our Lord endured. "Who (the Lord Jesus) for the joy that was set before him endured the cross, despising shame, and hath sat down at the right hand of the throne of God" (v. 2). The experience of believers can never be compared to that of the Lord. Our Lord, though despising the shame, endured the sufferings of the cross even unto blood. The believer's endurance of shame and suffering stops short of shedding of blood.

What should a Christian expect his life to be like? We must not give an improper hope to the brethren. We should show them that they will encounter many things in the future, but that in none of these things will God's purpose and meaning be lacking. Why should they have to endure many trials? Why should they brush up against many problems? What are these trials and difficulties actually for? What is the meaning of Christian suffering? Unless we are called to martyrdom, our resisting and striving against sin has not reached the point of shedding of blood. Nonetheless, we still resist.

Why should these things happen? "And ye have forgotten the exhortation which reasoneth with you as with sons, 'My son, regard not lightly the chastening of the Lord, nor faint when thou art reproved of him; for whom the Lord loveth he chasteneth, and scourgeth every son whom he receiveth' " (vv. 5–6).

The apostle quotes from Proverbs, chapter 3. He says we

must not despise the chastening of the Lord, nor should we faint under His reproof. Here he tells us there are two attitudes which believers need to maintain. When a person is in the process of passing through hardship, being under the chastening of the Lord, he may easily regard it lightly and let the chastisement of the Lord slip by. Or, when he is faced with the reproach of the Lord, the hand of the Lord being heavy upon him, he may faint, considering it too difficult to be a Christian. He expects to have a prosperous road in this life—to wear a white linen garment and walk leisurely on the golden street which leads to the pearly gate. He has never dreamed that to be a Christian means he will encounter so many troubles. Since he is not mentally prepared to be a Christian under such circumstances, he feels discouraged and thinks of quitting. But the book of Proverbs indicates that neither of these reactions is correct.

We should not despise the discipline of the Lord. If the Lord should chasten us, we need to be very serious about it. Whenever the Lord permits something to happen to us, He has His purpose behind it. He intends to use these happenings to edify us. All of His chastenings are to perfect us that we may be holier. He chastens us in order to make us partakers of His divine nature. The aim of discipline is to educate and train our character. The Lord never scourges us without a cause. He always has His mind set upon beating and shaping us into a vessel, never desiring just to make His children suffer. To suffer for the sake of suffering is not His way. If He allows us to suffer, He always has a motive behind it, and that is, He wants us to have a part in His holiness. This is the purpose of discipline.

It is, nevertheless, quite possible for children of God to

be Christians eight or ten years without ever having regarded God's chastisement seriously. They may never have acknowledged before the Lord, saying, "The Lord is chastening me; the Lord is dealing with me. He intends to beat me and fashion me into a vessel." Because they do not see the purpose behind God's scourging, His dealing and cutting, they let these chastenings slide past. They allow the things which happen to them day by day to simply pass by. They do not know what the purpose of the Lord is. Their attitude toward these things seems to imply that God is a God without purpose who simply leaves people to suffer. Therefore, the first attitude God's children need to learn is to take seriously the chastening of the Lord. Whenever something occurs, the first question should be, "What does this mean?" or, "Why is it so?" Learn to regard it seriously or else it will pass by without benefiting you.

We ought not to regard chastening lightly, but neither must we take it too hard. If to be a Christian means to suffer from morning till night, we could easily get disheartened. This is taking chastening too hard. What we need to do is to accept the Lord's discipline and understand its meaning.

The Nature of Discipline

"For whom the Lord loveth he chasteneth, and scourgeth every son whom he receiveth" (v. 6). This is quoted from Proverbs 3:12. It shows us the "why" of all chastenings.

God does not deal with everyone in the world. He only chastens those whom He loves. He chastens us because we are His beloved. He wants to make us into a suitable vessel. That is why He spends time on His children to chasten them. Chastisement, then, is love's arrangement. Love arranges these happenings. Love measures what we should meet. Love plans the details of our environment. We call this discipline because it always aims at the highest good and the ultimate intention of creation.

"And scourgeth every son whom he receiveth." Those who are chastened of the Lord are those who are assuredly accepted by God. To be scourged is not a sign of rejection, but rather the evidence of God's special approval. God does not deal with everyone; He just concentrates on dealing with those whom He loves, those who are accepted as His sons.

As a Christian, you must be ready to receive God's chastening. If you are not a child of God, He will let you go your way and live your careless life. But once you accept the Lord Jesus as your Savior and are born of God, you become a child of God; thus you need to be ready to accept discipline. A father does not try to scourge other peoples' sons; whether the neighbor's son is good or bad is none of his business. But a good father does pay close attention to educate his own son. There are certain things in which he will deal strictly with his son; they are not incidentals which can be casually taught. The father himself must decide in which things he will instruct his son. He will want his son to learn honesty, diligence, endurance, and high ideals. The father, as it were, plans the curriculum of instruction so as to make his son the kind of person he wants him to be. Likewise, from the time you are saved, God has arranged a curriculum for you that you may learn to be a partaker of His nature. There are certain respects in which He wants you to be as He is. So He arranges these chastenings and scourgings.

Therefore, at the outset a Christian should be shown that a child of God needs to accept all the lessons that God has prepared for him. God has arranged all kinds of environments, all sorts of happenings, and many sufferings with a view to creating in His child a certain nature and character. This is what God wants to do. Because of His desire to create a certain character in you, God arranges your environment for you.

After you become a Christian, you will see the hand of God leading you. Many prearranged things will happen to you. Scourgings will come too. Why the scourgings? Because whenever you are not walking in God's appointed way, you will be scourged and urged to turn from that direction back to the appointed road. Every child of God must be prepared to accept this disciplinary hand of God. Because you are His son, He chastens you. If you are not His beloved, He will not make the effort to discipline you. Thus, to be chastened and scourged is an indication that we are loved and accepted by God. Only Christians share in His chastening and scourging.

What we receive is not punishment but discipline. Punishment serves the purpose of repaying the wrong, but discipline has an educational purpose. Punishment deals only with the past—one is scourged because he has done wrong. Discipline has an eye toward the future though it also deals with past faults. Discipline, therefore, has these two elements—an educational purpose as training for the future. As soon as one comes to Christ and belongs to the Lord, he should be prepared to let God mold him into a vessel of honor. I can say with confidence that God wants to make every child of His glorify Him in some certain respect. All Christians shall glorify Him, but it will be in a different area for each one. Some glorify Him in one way, and some in another way. He is to be glorified in all kinds of situations that He may get a perfect glory. Each person glorifies God with his particular portion—something in his character that the Lord has formed in him. This is the outcome of the disciplinary hand of God upon him. For this reason, it is absolutely impossible for a child of God not to have God's hand upon him.

It is a great loss to those who do not understand the discipline of God. Quite frankly, many live so foolishly before God for so many years that they become people without a way. They do not know what the Lord is doing with them. Therefore they live according to their own whims, having none of the Lord's restraint. They run wild as in a wilderness with no destination in view. This is not God's way. He has a definite purpose—to develop in us a special character, a character which will glorify His name. All of His chastenings lead us to this road.

The Contents of Discipline

When the apostle wrote to the Hebrews, he quoted the words in Proverbs. Starting from verse 7 in Hebrews 12, he tried to explain the quotation, "It is for chastening that ye endure." The New Testament interprets the Old Testament. The interpretation here is extremely important for the apostle shows us that suffering and chastening (or discipline) are one and the same thing. What we endure is God's discipline.

Some may ask, what is the discipline of God? Verses 2 through 4 mention despising shame, enduring the suffering of the cross and striving against sin, while verses 5 and 6 talk about discipline and scourging. What is the connection between these two portions? What is this discipline and scourging? What is meant by shame, suffering, and striving? Simply remember that verse 7 gathers up verses 2 to 6 by showing us that what we endure is the discipline of God. Hence, suffering is God's discipline; enduring shame is God's discipline; striving against sin though not yet unto blood is also God's discipline.

How does God discipline us? Whatever God has led you through, whatever He has permitted you to endure—this is His discipline. Do not imagine that His discipline is something special. No, the discipline of God is found in that which you endure every day—a hard word, a bad face, a sharp tongue, discourteous treatment, an unreasonable criticism, an unexpected happening, various kinds of disgrace, irresponsibility on the part of family members—all the many pains and difficulties you meet, large or small. Sometimes you have to endure sicknesses, deprivations, distresses, and difficulties. All these are the discipline of God; what you endure, says the apostle, is God's discipline.

The problem then is: If a person turns a bad face to me, what will my reaction be? Is not this bad face the discipline of God? How will I treat the person who ruins my affair because of his poor memory? If this poor memory is God's discipline, how will I treat him? If my illness is caused by contagion, how will I react? If my failure is due to misfortune, what will I say? If these things are due to God's discipline, what shall I say? Brothers and sisters, these things make a big difference. Do not think that the various things you encounter in your environment are incidental and thus in attitude regard them as insignificant. If you could see that these are all God's disciplines, your attitude would definitely be different. It is quite clear from the words of the apostle that what you endure is the discipline of the Lord. Therefore, you should never conclude that the things you are going through are unbearable. Also, do not ignorantly regard them as accidental. You should know better: these things are arranged daily for you by God. They are His measured discipline for you.

"God dealeth with you as with sons; for what son is there whom his father chasteneth not?" (v. 7). All these chastenings come upon us because God treats us as His own sons. Do remember: discipline is God's favor, not His animosity. Many have the wrong idea that when they are disciplined they are being ill-treated by God. No, God treats us like sons. Is there any son whom the father does not discipline? In disciplining you, God is favoring you! Because you have become God's children, you are disciplined. He wants to bring you to the place of blessing and of glory.

Here is the great divide. When one realizes that his daily happenings come from God, his whole attitude toward these events changes. Supposing someone comes up and tries to whip me. If I struggle with him, break the whip, and throw it in his face, I owe him nothing. But if that man is my father, would I do those things? No, for in a father's beating we oftentimes can sense that which is precious. Madame Guyon once said, "I will kiss the whip that beats me; I will kiss the hand that strikes me." What a difference it makes if you remember that this is the father's hand and the father's whip. If it were just an ordinary occurrence, you might feel fretful. But this is not ordinary, for it is God's hand and God's whip. Its aim is to make you a partaker of His nature and of His character. Having seen this, you can neither complain nor fret. Once you know it is of the Father, this thing has changed its color. To be disciplined by God is a glorious experience.

"But if ye are without chastening, whereof all have been made partakers, then are ye bastards, and not sons" (v. 8). Discipline is the proof that we are sons. Who are the sons of God? Those who are disciplined of God. Who are not God's sons? Those who are not disciplined. He who is not disciplined has no proof of being a son. The evidence of being a son lies in discipline.

Discipline is shared by all the sons. You, too, are not an exception. If you are not a bastard but a son, then you will have to share in the discipline. The word of the apostle is very emphatic, "Whereof all have been made partakers." As a son of God, do not hope for any different treatment. Discipline is shared by all God's sons. All who live today fare the same way as those who lived in the time of Peter and Paul. There is no exception whatever. How can you expect to travel a course which no child of God has ever traveled, a course void of God's discipline? Can a child of God be so foolish as to dream of a prosperous life and work without any discipline of God? You can easily see that such a one must be a bastard. Discipline, we now see, is a signal of being God's child, the evidence thereof. Lack of discipline reveals those who are bastards, those who do not belong to God's house.

I once witnessed a scene which may serve as a good illustration: I saw five or six children playing in the yard. They were all covered with mud. A mother came and boxed the ears of three of the children, forbidding them to continue playing. One child exclaimed, "Why don't you strike those others too?" "Because they are not my children," replied the mother. Do you see, no parent wants to chasten other people's children. Woe to us if God does not scourge us. The undisciplined are bastards, not sons.

Since you are believers, you will receive discipline from the very beginning of your Christian life. Who can receive sonship and reject discipline? These two go together. All sons are disciplined and you are no exception.

Our Attitude toward Discipline

"Furthermore, we had the fathers of our flesh to chasten us, and we gave them reverence: shall we not much rather be in subjection unto the Father of spirits, and live?" (v. 9). The apostle shows us that if we reverence our fathers in the flesh when they discipline us, acknowledging that such discipline is right and, therefore, accepting it, how much more we should be in subjection to the Father of spirits and live.

In sonship, we find discipline; and in discipline, we find subjection. Because we are sons, we will be disciplined; since we are disciplined, we must be in subjection. Remember, whatever God arranges in our environment is for the purpose of instructing and directing us in the straight path.

We must obey God. We must obey these two things He gives: first, His command; and second, His chastening. On the one hand, we obey God's word, obey His command, and obey all the precepts given us in the Bible. On the other hand, we subject ourselves to all God's arrangements in our environment; we are in subjection to all the discipline of God. Though our obedience to God's word may be sufficient, we often may yet be lacking in subjection to God's discipline. Since He has so ordered that such a thing should happen to you, you ought to be benefited by it and learn the lesson. God wants you to be benefited and to walk in the straight path. We must, therefore, learn not only to obey the Lord's command but also to obey the Lord's discipline. Although it costs us to obey the Lord's discipline, it nonetheless enables us to walk straightforwardly before God.

But obedience is not an empty word. Numbers of brothers have asked me: what do you want me to obey? This is easily answered. Do you think there is nothing to be obeyed? Let me tell you, should God only discipline you half a day, you would probably already think of escaping! It is rather strange that some brothers find nothing to obey. What He wants you to obey is His disciplinary hand upon you.

Why do we not speak of God's *guiding hand* instead of His *disciplinary hand?* Why do we not say that the Lord leads me instead of saying that God disciplines me? The reason is that God knows us too well. He knows that apart from discipline many will never really learn obedience.

You need to know what kind of a person you are before God. Our natural inclination is toward rebellion and obstinacy. We are like naughty children; we will not listen unless we see the rod in the father's hand. Indeed, we all are alike in this respect. Discipline is absolutely necessary for us. Let us therefore know ourselves. We are not as simple as we suppose ourselves to be. Even after a beating, we may yet be disobedient. The apostle shows us that scourging is to help us to hearken and to obey. "Shall we not much rather be in subjection unto the Father of Spirits, and live?" Subjection is indispensable. Learn to obey God, saying, "O God, I am willing to be in subjection to your discipline, for whatever you do is right."

The Purpose of Discipline

"For they indeed for a few days chastened us as seemed good to them" (v. 10a). When parents discipline their children, they reveal much deficiency, for they chasten according to their own thoughts. Consequently, the profit from such discipline is only a little. "But he for our profit, that we may be partakers of his holiness" (v. 10b). The discipline of God neither issues from temper nor is it for punishment. All the discipline of God is educational; it is given for our profit. Scourging is not administered just for pain, but the pain is meant to produce some positive value. Pain has its purpose; it is not mere punishment for some fault. If one thinks in terms of punishment, it shows that his mind is yet under the bondage of law.

What is the profit? It is that we may be partakers of His holiness. This, indeed, is most glorious. Holiness is God's nature. We may say that holiness is God's character. It is for this reason that God uses all kinds of ways to chasten His children. From the very start of our Christian life, God chastens us with persistency. He has one purpose in mind, that is, He wants us to be partakers of His holy character.

Holiness in the Bible has various shades of meaning. For instance, the Bible teaches us that Christ is our righteousness and that we are sanctified in Christ; this gives us a different picture from what we have here in the book of Hebrews. Here, holiness is not something given but something fashioned. It fits in with the word "incorporated" which we have emphasized these many years. Holiness is that which God gradually works into us or slowly incorporates in us. Through His discipline, by His scourging, He daily incorporates His holiness in us. The aim of all these chastenings and works is to make us partakers of His holiness.

After each scourging, I learn and partake a little bit more of His holiness. Under His discipline, I come to see what holiness is. As I am constantly under His discipline, my character is gradually built up in holiness; that is, my character is transformed. Let me tell you, there is nothing greater than this work. I want you all to know that through discipline God's character is built in us. Each stroke of discipline has its value. We may derive fruit from every instance of discipline. I beseech God to be merciful to me that, whenever I am chastened, something more of holiness may be produced in me. May each chastening cause me to learn more of holiness and to incorporate in me more of His holiness. May holiness always be on the increase!

After one has received the Lord and become a child of God, he will meet with many disciplines and scourgings day after day by God's special arrangements. These are precious lessons. By these lessons, God's holiness is to be incorporated little by little in us. It takes a great deal of discipline to produce a holy character. We may not be many decades on this earth. If we waste God's disciplines and let them pass by unprofitably, what an eternal loss it will be!

God has not only given us His holiness, He will also incorporate His holiness in us through discipline. Little by little He works holiness into us. For such carnal people as we are, it really needs many years of chastening to produce in us His holy character. How many beatings, how many arrangements, how many leadings, how many restraints as well as constraints are required to gradually work holiness into us. What a great thing this is! Holiness is not simply given to us like a gift; it is to be produced in us. God is producing His holiness in us!

This is a prime characteristic of New Testament salvation. God not only *has* once given salvation to us, but, after He has given it, He starts to build it in us through patient inworking. By joining these two processes together, we see full salvation. The one comes from the gift of Christ; the other is built through the incorporation of the Holy Spirit. One is given, the other is built. It is God who builds holiness in us. One of the important words of the New Testament is that through discipline we may be partakers of His holiness.

The Fruit of Discipline

"All chastening seemeth for the present to be not joyous but grievous; yet afterward it yieldeth peaceable fruit unto them that have been exercised thereby, even the fruit of righteousness" (v. 11). The apostle draws our attention to the "afterward" as well as the "present." It is a fact that for the present all discipline is not joyous but grievous. When you are faced with God's discipline, there is nothing wrong with feeling sorrowful. You should feel pained. The Bible has not said that the cross is joyous; it states instead that the cross is suffering. The cross causes us to suffer. It is true that our Lord, for the joy which was set before Him, despised the shame, but the Bible never describes the cross as joyous. The cross is not joyous, but grievous. When you are under discipline, you feel grieved. It is right for you to feel that way.

However, this is the time to learn obedience in order that you may be made partaker of God's holiness. During the period of the discipline, you cannot but feel grieved, even as our Lord felt when He passed through trials. But at the same time, you may count it as joy even as our Lord did. Does not Peter say, "Wherein ye greatly rejoice, though now for a little while, if need be, ye have been put to grief in manifold trials" (1 Pet. 1:6)? It is all right for you to feel grieved, but you also may count it as joy. To feel is one thing, to count is another thing. You do not feel joyous, but you may count it as joy.

A child of God should not always look at the present but rather at that which will follow. Notice these words: "All chastening seemeth for the present to be not joyous but grievous; yet afterward it yieldeth peaceable fruit unto them that have been exercised thereby, even the fruit of righteousness." Do not be occupied with how much you are suffering now but rather look forward to the peaceful fruit of righteousness.

"Moab hath been at ease from his youth, and he hath settled on his lees, and hath not been emptied from vessel to vessel, neither hath he gone into captivity: therefore his taste remaineth in him, and his scent is not changed" (Jer. 48:11).

This is exactly the problem with many who have not gone through trials or been chastened by God. Moab has been at ease from his youth. He has not experienced any trial or pain. Such an easy life makes him like wine which has settled on its dregs. The wine is on the top, but the dregs are at the bottom. To thoroughly strain the wine, you need to pour it from vessel to vessel. Otherwise, the dregs at the bottom will later on affect the taste of the wine. In making wine, you first ferment the grapes or whatever raw materials you are using. After fermentation, you empty the wine from one vessel to another. You need to exercise extreme care in doing this lest the dregs also be emptied. And you must pour the wine again and again from vessel to vessel till there is no sediment left in the vessel. But Moab, God said, has been at ease from his youth. He has settled on his lees; he has not been emptied from vessel to vessel. Therefore his dregs follow him. Moab is full of dregs. Though the top part is pure, the bottom part has never been emptied. Those who have not gone through trials and chastening are like wine which has never been emptied from vessel to vessel.

When a condition such as this exists, God may have to pull the person up by his roots. Sometimes this is done through consecration. Sometimes it is brought about by suffering, trials, or sickness. This is what is meant by being emptied from vessel to vessel. The hand of God is upon you; He wants you to be utterly broken. As a consequence, your dregs are strained out. Moab has never been emptied, hence his dregs are with him.

Hence, to live an easy life is not really a good thing. Brothers and sisters, God disciplines us because He wants to purify us. He scourges us in order to cleanse us. Do not seek for ease and comfort. Moab's ease transfixed him to forever remain as Moab. "Therefore his taste remaineth in him, and his scent is not changed." Since he had never been emptied from vessel to vessel, since he had never been chastened by God, his taste remained in him and his scent was not changed.

Brethren, this is why God is working. He is working to take away your original taste and to change your original scent. He does not want your taste and scent. Occasionally I have said that many Christians are yet "raw" people because their original condition has never been changed. Before you believed in the Lord you had a certain taste; but now it has been ten years since you believed, and that taste remains the same. Your scent has not changed since you became a Christian. This means that God has not been able to incorporate, fashion, and work Himself into you.

God's discipline is indeed most precious. He will uproot us, He will empty us from vessel to vessel. He will give us many chastenings and many dealings in order to get rid of our original taste and to get us to produce peaceable fruit, the fruit of righteousness.

I like the words "peaceable fruit" for it is only when a person is peaceful before God that he produces fruit. What we should fear to do is to complain, fret, and become insubordinate under discipline. To feel grieved is permissible, but to murmur and disobey ought not to happen. I notice that those who complain are those who lack peace. It is necessary, therefore, to have the peaceable fruit in chastening. How can one produce peaceable fruit? First, by learning to accept God's discipline and not arguing or quarreling with God. Peaceable fruit is the fruit of righteousness. When peace is with you, righteousness will issue forth. This is truly remarkable. When a person is not peaceful before God and starts talking, he instantly loses righteousness. For where there is talking, there is conflict. Peace is silent.

Therefore, learn to be subject to discipline, for it will produce peaceable fruit. Tell the Lord that His chastening cannot be wrong, that what has happened is just what you need. Tell Him that you will be submissive. This will then become your peaceable fruit, out of which will issue forth the fruit of righteousness. Peace is righteousness. If your inward fruit is peace, your outward manifestation will be righteousness.

Let us hope that we are not like Moab who has been at ease from his youth and has settled on his lees. He has not been poured from vessel to vessel, nor has he been in captivity. Hence, his taste remains with him and his scent is not changed. Some Christians are like Moab. Though they have been Christians for ten, twenty, or more years, they have yet to truly accept any of God's dealings. Because they have never been obedient to any of God's dealings over these years, their taste remains the same as before. Should such be our case, we will never bear peaceable fruit before God. Consequently, we will not have the holy character which God intends to build in us.

A Final Word

"Wherefore, lift up the hands that hang down, and the palsied knees" (v. 12). Under discipline, the hands are inclined to hang down and the knees be palsied. But the apostle exhorts us not to faint, for however drooping our hands are and however feeble our knees are, there is still the peaceable fruit of righteousness.

Do not feel discouraged and think that after all the trials and chastenings you have gone through there is nothing left of you. Lift up your drooping hands and straighten your feeble knees because discipline and scourging have produced in you the peaceable fruit which is the fruit of righteousness. If you have peace before God, you also have righteousness. If you can be quiet before God, then it is well. If you can be submissive, then His holy character is being built in you. You need not look for righteousness; you only need to look for peace and subjection and tenderness before God. If you have been tender, obedient, and peaceful, holiness will be your share. Do remember: although you have endured many trials and encountered many hardships in the past, you should lift up your drooping hands and straighten your feeble knees today.

Meanwhile, "Make straight paths for your feet, that that which is lame be not turned out of the way, but rather be healed" (v. 13). After you yourself have gone through this way, you then can present a straight path to others that even the lame be not turned aside but rather be healed. Those who cannot walk will be able to walk with you because you have made the way straight. Simply remember this: if, when in trials, you humble yourself under the mighty hand of God, not only will the holy character of God be built in you but also you will be able to lead others to walk uprightly.

If the person who walks in front deviates a little, he may take the straight path away from others. For this reason, we must be obedient, we must produce the peaceable fruit of righteousness. Thus not only will our path be straight but also we may lead others to walk in the straight path too. Then the lame shall not be turned out of the way but shall be healed. This reminds me of the lame person in Acts 3 and of how his feet and his ankle bones received strength. "And leaping up, he stood, and began to walk; and he entered with them into the temple, walking, and leaping and praising God" (v. 8). This lame person was healed. There are many other lame ones also who need to be healed. May we open the way for our brethren.

RESIST THE DEVIL

Be sober, be watchful: your adversary the devil, as a roaring lion, walketh about, seeking whom he may devour: whom withstand stedfast in your faith, knowing that the same sufferings are accomplished in your brethren who are in the world.

1 Pet. 5:8–9

That no advantage may be gained over us by Satan: for we are not ignorant of his devices.

2 Cor. 2:11

These two scriptural passages indicate to us how full of evil devices Satan is. His basic work is to camouflage whatever he does so that people will not know it is his doing! He even fashions himself into an angel of light (2 Cor. 11:14). All his works are done under the cover of deceit. When he speaks a lie, he speaks of his own: for he is a liar and he always lies (John 8:44). Of all that he has ever done, he has never willingly and openly acknowledged anything as his work. If he were to make a public report of his works, probably nobody would want them; everyone would probably resist them. For this reason, he always disguises his work in a multitude of ways.

The Work of Satan

Satan's works are manifold. In order for a Christian to walk well before God, he must learn how to resist Satan. In order to do that, he must discern what is the work of Satan. According to the judgment of the Bible, many so-called natural things are actually Satanic works. From a human point of view we may consider something to be incidental, natural, or circumstantial, but the Bible distinctly labels it as the work of the devil. If we are to follow a straight course, God's children must not be ignorant of the devices of Satan—how full of wiles he is, how pretentious and deceptive. We should recognize him in order to resist him.

1. THE WORK OF SATAN IN THE HUMAN MIND

Let us now mention a few of Satan's devices so that we may resist him and overcome him before the Lord.

"For the weapons of our warfare are not of the flesh, but mighty before God to the casting down of strongholds; casting down imaginations, and every high thing that is exalted against the knowledge of God, and bringing every thought into captivity to the obedience of Christ" (2 Cor. 10:4–5). Satan surrounds man with strongholds so as to prevent him from obeying Christ. The special field of his work is found in man's mind or thought life. Oftentimes man is bombarded with speculations or imaginations which are adverse to the obedience of Christ. Paul says the weapons of our warfare against these are not of the flesh. These imaginations must first be destroyed before we can bring our thoughts into captivity to the obedience of Christ.

The sphere of Satan's operation is in man's thought life.

He will inject a thought, an imagination, which appears to be your own. Under this deception, you accept it and use it as if it were yours, though in actuality it is his.

Do remember that many things in the life of a Christian begin with speculations or imaginations. Many sins are first committed in the imagination of the mind. Many unpleasantnesses among brothers and sisters arise from these fancies.

Then there are those sudden thoughts. Sometimes a thought will flash into one's mind that a certain brother is wrong. Many of God's children do not recognize such thoughts as the work of Satan. A person may consider such a thought as his own and take it as true, thinking that the brother really is wrong. And yet, this is not true. It is Satan who has put the thought into his mind. How is he to resist the devil? He must say, "I do not want this thought. I return it to you, Satan." Should he accept it, it will become his own thought. It is Satan's at the start, but it will become his if he keeps it.

Christians need to know what Satanic temptation is. Satanic temptation enters mainly, if not exclusively, in the form of thought. When Satan tempts people, he does not attach a label saying, "This is Satanic temptation!" If people knew it was of Satan they would resist it. No, he sneaks in stealthily without causing a ripple. All his temptations are formulated so as not to easily arouse the Christians. He does not want them to suspect him; he would rather have them sleep on. So he surreptitiously injects a thought into their mind. Once they accept it, it has become a foothold for him.

This is why the children of God must learn how to resist inordinate thoughts. However, they also should be careful lest they become overly attentive. Any excess in this respect will cause further confusion of the thoughts, causing them to fall further into the wiles of the enemy. If one is concentrating on his thoughts, his eyes will not be focusing on the Lord. We must, indeed, resist improper thoughts, yet we should not be wholly occupied with our thoughts.

I would like to cry aloud that over these years I have seen two extremes: some people exercise no restraint in their thoughts, others are totally taken up with dealing with their thoughts. The latter are just as deceived by Satan as the former. Further, they are likely candidates for a nervous breakdown. So we need to maintain the right balance. We should not allow Satan to tempt us by injecting his thoughts; neither should we be engrossed in how to deal with our thoughts. If we are constantly taken up with dealing with our thoughts, then we have fallen into Satan's temptation, for, instead of having our eyes on the Lord, they are on our thoughts.

Satanic thoughts can be quite easily withstood. There is a saying frequently quoted by many servants of the Lord that goes, "You cannot forbid a bird to fly over your head, but you certainly can forbid it to make a nest in your hair." Do remember, then, that though you cannot prohibit many thoughts from passing through your mind, you can prohibit them from nesting in you. As a thought flashes through you, you may thrust it away by simply saying, "I do not want it. I will not accept it. I reject it." Then you will see that it is thrown out.

Many of God's children have great difficulty with their thoughts. They cannot easily control them. Of the many letters I have received over these past years, the one question most frequently asked is, "How can I control my thoughts?" Some confess that they find it especially difficult to control their thoughts during their prayer time. At this point there is something I would like to say briefly. "Finally, brethren, whatsoever things are true, whatsoever things are honorable, whatsoever things are just, whatsoever things are pure, whatsoever things are lovely, whatsoever things are of good report; if there be any virtue, and if there be any praise, think on these things" (Phil. 4:8), the Bible tells us. Think on these things! God's children should learn to engage their thoughts in positive thinking. The more they use their mind positively, the less their thoughts will be out of control. Many are not able to control their thoughts because they do not think; they are passive in their thought life. This gives Satan the opportunity to insert some of his many ready-made thoughts into their minds.

Satan will not find it so easy to inject his thought into your mind if you learn to use your mind for thinking on things spiritual, good, righteous, holy, peaceful, and loveable. When your mind is positively engaged and your thoughts are not idle, Satan has no opportunity. But if a Christian's mind is unoccupied and idle, then that passive, ungirded mind of his is open to Satanic infiltration.

Because of this, God's children ought to exercise their minds as they exercise their bodies. This will prevent the intrusion of Satanic thoughts. Learn to recognize what thoughts are unclean, divisive, and slanderous, and then learn to resist them as soon as they are discovered to be of the enemy. Many thoughts are distinctly Satanic and therefore can be easily rejected. Some thoughts, though, are quite subtle and therefore not so easily repudiated. Nonetheless, we must learn to resist all of them.

Satan is neither omniscient nor omnipresent. He is, however, acquainted with many things, for through his evil spirits—the sinful angels—he has spread an intelligence network throughout the earth. When we are idle, Satan easily puts something that is known to him, but not to us, into our thought. He injects the intelligence that his secret service has obtained into our thoughts. He makes us fancy something, imagine something, and thus thrusts his intelligence into our mind. As soon as we ponder it and accept it, it becomes real to us. God's children, therefore, must reject all communications from Satan, even if such communications do shed light on things. We should refuse to know anything that does not come to our knowledge by revelation received through prayer.

A child of God must not be curious or nosy. If he is not, he will escape many Satanic thoughts. If he is, Satan will supply him endlessly with some of the many things he knows. The Christian at first may think that such knowledge is beneficial. However, if he continues to accept these thoughts, he will soon become a pawn in Satan's hand. Satan will employ the Christian's mind to do his work. It is for this reason that one must resist all causeless thoughts. Whenever a thought about another brother's fault flashes into one's mind, if it comes from the thought of the mind and not from the consciousness of the Spirit, it should be rejected. If it is accepted, it will eventually become a personal conviction. One who thinks a brother has done him wrong will soon reckon it to be real. Consequently, he will break fellowship with his brother.

Unless these sudden thoughts are cut off at the beginning, they will get out of hand afterward. When Satanic temptations first invade the mind, they are relatively easy to deal with; but once they become "facts" in the mind, they are most difficult to get rid of. For this reason we must deal with thoughts. We must reject all unclean thoughts lest we sin. We must actively use our mind so as not to live a loose and dissipated life. Under God's light, we shall see that many sins come through receiving temptations in the thought life.

Let me reiterate: after a thought is first resisted, the matter is considered closed. When the thought comes the second time, it should be ignored. In other words, when a thought first comes to you, resist it by faith, believing that it has fled away. Should it present itself the second time, it comes as a lie, not the truth. Therefore, you must reckon it as false and declare that you have already resisted it. Take this position until the thought flees. If you acknowledge the returned thought as true, you shall soon find it so attached to you that you can hardly throw it off. Many defeats may be attributed to this error. If you resist the devil, he will flee from you. This is the word of the Lord and it is totally trustworthy. Whatever Satan says is undependable. The Lord says, "Resist the devil, and he will flee from you" (Jas. 4:7). Therefore, that which comes back again must be a fake and should be totally discredited.

Why are the minds of so many Christians confused? It is because they are always resisting. "Resist the devil, and he will flee from you," says the Bible. Resist him once, and he will flee. You ought to believe that he has fled away. You do not need to resist him many times. Simply believe that he has fled, for this is in accordance with God's Word. Whatever then comes back is not true. You can well afford to ignore it, and, if you do, it will soon disappear. It lurks just outside the door, trying to peep in; if you reckon it as true, it will immediately step in. So, the basic principle is: resist the first time, ignore the second time. If a second time indeed comes, you do not even need to resist; all that

51

is necessary is to not pay the slightest attention. To resist the second time is to discredit the first resistance; to resist the third time is to refute the first and the second resistances, and so on. Each new resistance means one more distrust of your former resistance. Because you do not believe what the Lord has said, "Resist the devil, and he will flee from you," you resist to the hundredth time. You will be occupied with resisting from dawn to dusk. The more you think, the more confused you become. The more you use your mind, the more severely you suffer. Therefore, do not resist foolishly. Simply believe that once resisted the devil will flee.

2. THE WORK OF SATAN ON MAN'S BODY

Satan sometimes works upon the human mind and sometimes on man's body. Many sicknesses are not real sicknesses, but are actually Satanic works. Sometimes illnesses are manifestly Satanic attacks.

When Peter's mother-in-law was laid aside with a severe fever, the Lord Jesus went to the house and rebuked the fever (Lk. 4:39). Fever is simply a symptom; it has no personality. You cannot rebuke a symptom; you can only rebuke a personality. You cannot rebuke a chair or a watch, for neither of them has a personality. You only rebuke that which has a personality. But here the Lord Jesus did a surprising thing. When He saw Peter's mother-in-law ill with a fever, He rebuked the fever and it subsided. This clearly indicates that the fever was not ordinary, that it possessed a personality. In other words, it was the work of Satan. At the rebuke of the Lord, Satan retreated.

Another instance is shown in the healing of a child who was deaf and dumb from childhood (Mk. 9:17, 21, 25–27).

When the father of the child brought him to the Lord Jesus, the Lord rebuked the unclean spirit saying, "Thou dumb and deaf spirit, I command thee, come out of him, and enter no more into him." And the child was healed. The sickness had been caused by an evil spirit. At the rebuke of the Lord, the evil spirit came out of the child, and the child regained his speech and hearing.

Thus we find two different kinds of patients in the New Testament: the medically or physiologically sick, and those who are sick because of Satan's attack. The first kind of patient the Lord healed; the second kind, since the sickness had a personality, He rebuked.

Many sicknesses are indeed physical ailments, but many are the results of Satanic attacks on the body. God's children need to learn how to resist this latter kind.

Sometimes you cannot understand why you are sick. You have not been careless; so far as you know there has been no possibility of contagion for this particular sickness in your immediate environment. Yet you are sick. You are suddenly incapacitated when you have something of God's work or some spiritual thing to do. This sickness is not ordinary since it cannot be attributed to any natural cause. Furthermore, you became sick just at the time when you had some spiritual work to fulfill. With your eyes closed you can almost judge that this sickness is due to Satanic assault.

This kind of sickness will disappear if you resist it before the Lord, saying, "Lord, I do not accept this sickness, for it comes from the enemy!" Most amazing, you will find that it goes away as suddenly as it came. Neither its coming nor its going can be attributed to any natural cause. It leaves under rebuke.

Take Job as an example. Here was a man who was

attacked by Satan with sore boils from the sole of his feet to the crown of his head. Satan aimed at killing him, but God obstructed the devil's intention by decreeing: "Spare his life."

We Christians need to have a different view of sickness. Many sicknesses are not real sicknesses but are the works of Satan. Many weaknesses are due to the acceptance of Satanic works which, unfortunately, have never been questioned. We must learn this lesson before God: whenever we are sick, we should examine the cause. We should inquire whether the sickness has a proper cause. If a reasonable doubt arises, we should investigate further. We must not accept *any* sickness without questioning. It may be a real sickness or it may be a Satanic attack. If the latter is the case, we need to resist by declaring that we will not accept what Satan has put on us.

If God's children will stand up and resist, many sicknesses will soon disappear. I do not dare to say that all sickness is attributable to Satan, but I do believe that many sicknesses are caused by his attack. And because these are not questioned and resisted, such sicknesses succeed in making people really ill. If they were resisted, Satan would fail in his work and such illnesses would be eliminated. Is this not wonderful?

Permit me to mention a little of my own experience, though I am most reluctant to refer to things too personal. It happened in 1928 or 1929. I returned to Foochow from Shanghai. For more than two days I ran a high fever of 105° to 106° F. I was staying with a relative, and I felt uneasy about troubling her. I did not know what caused the sickness. I was greatly confused by the many thoughts which crowded into my mind. I was so desperate that finally I managed to get out of bed and sit on the porch.

"O Lord, I have to know what is the matter," I prayed. At that moment, I was either praying or reading the Bible. Suddenly it dawned on me that probably this was Satan's attack, for it bore no resemblance to the Lord's hand upon me. As soon as the light came that this was the work of Satan, my inward being was wonderfully enlightened and freed. I had never thought about this being Satan's attack. Suddenly I became wise and saw through the symptom. So I declared that since this was Satan's work, I would not accept it; rather, I would resist it. I was quite uncomfortable that night and struggled much. But I did have a little light within, showing me that this came from the enemy. I resisted and refused to accept it. The next morning I slept a little, and after that the sickness was gone. I did not know how the fever left me. Since then I have had many such experiences in my life. I trust that many other brothers and sisters will have similar experiences. Rebuke Satan, and the sickness will subside.

The experiences of many bear witness to the fact that if a sickness is accepted it will continue, but if it is rejected it will be terminated. Naturally, this does not refer to all sicknesses. What is important, then, is to receive light from God to discern whether or not the attack is of Satan. If it is a Satanic attack, then it must be caused by that which is supernatural instead of being naturally reasonable. Once it is recognized as Satanic, resist it, and it shall fade away.

Satan desires not only a believer's sickness but even his death. Being a murderer from the beginning, he conspires to bring about the premature death of many, especially of God's children. Therefore, before God we must resist Satan's murderous design. We need to resist him not only as a devil but also as a murderer. Too many of the children of God have the mistaken notion that it would be good if they died. No, such a thought comes from the enemy, for he is always plotting against human life. We can see his evil intention to murder in his insidious attack on Job.

Do not accept the thought of death. It comes from Satan. Perhaps a sudden thought flashes into your mind to put yourself into a dangerous position while you are walking on the street, riding in a boat, or boarding an airplane. You are tempted to accept that thought of possible death. No, learn to reject it and resist it. At no time should you allow Satan to put such a thought into your mind.

A story was told of a believer who had the thought of cutting his throat whenever he was shaving. As a result, he dared not shave for fear that something terrible would happen. One day he told his fear to another brother who warned him that he should resist, for the thought clearly came from Satan. The first brother asked the other brother to pray for him. The latter replied that he would, but that still it must be the first brother who did the resisting. He advised his brother who had this fear to declare: "I resist any thought of death! In the name of the Lord Jesus, I cast out such a thought!"

You should not turn your back on Satan, for this will mean *you* are running away instead of *him* running away from you! You should face him and let him turn his back. If you are facing his back, it means he is running. But if you turn back from facing him, you are defeated. Declare that you will not commit suicide. If you do this, then you are facing him, and he will have to run away. If you tremble for fear you will kill yourself, then you are the one who is running away. If you are afraid of him, you are finished!

One day that brother who was fearful lest he might cut himself to death while shaving faced Satan and declared: "I was deceived by you. I know now that it was your doing. Today I resist you." Thereafter that thought never came back. Later he testified, saying, "Since the day I resisted, I have not even had a small cut while shaving." Do not think this is a small matter. Many are those who are under the greatest bondage in the smallest things. Learn, therefore, to recognize before God what Satan can do to the body. Whenever his attack is discerned, resist it until it disappears.

3. THE ACCUSATION OF SATAN IN THE CONSCIENCE

Satan not only attacks the mind and the body but also the conscience. This attack is what we call accusation. It causes great distress to the Christian who feels himself at fault and thus unable to rise up before God.

Accusation may weaken one's whole being. Many dare not resist for fear that it may be the reproof of the Holy Spirit. They cannot distinguish Satanic accusation from the reproach of the Holy Spirit. Hence they accept Satan's accusation as the Holy Spirit's reproach. Consequently, their lives are wasted under accusation. Do remember that Satanic accusation may cripple the most spiritual and most useful person and reduce him to nought. A weakened conscience weakens the entire person.

What is the difference between a conscience under accusation and the reproach of the Holy Spirit? It is extremely important that we know the difference. Satan's accusation is never clear and sharp, whereas the revelation from God distinctly places your sin before you. Far from being distinct, Satan's accusation is that which is continually mumbling. It is said in Proverbs that, "the contentions of a wife are a continuous dropping" (Prov. 19:13). Satanic accusation also operates somewhat like that. It comes down in two or three drops at a time, instead of a pouring out of the whole bucket of water at once. Satan's accusation babbles long like a talkative and dissatisfied woman. Her nature is such that she will not speak out clearly but she will murmur incessantly so as to leave you with a guilty feeling. So is Satanic accusation. It never comes out boldly but rather mumbles along till you feel greatly distressed. When the Holy Spirit comes, though, He enlightens you with a great light so that you distinctly see your fault.

Furthermore, Satanic accusation lacks positive purpose. It does not edify you but, instead, causes you to suffer. It mumbles till it affects you and so overwhelms you that you are no longer able to stand up before God. The purpose of the reproach of the Holy Spirit, however, is to strengthen you, not to weaken you. The more you are reproved, the easier for you to rise up before God. Satanic accusation produces the opposite effect: the more you are accused, the more you are weakened. Hence the reproach of the Holy Spirit is positive in nature. He so reproves that you have to go to the Lord and learn your lesson. Satanic accusation is quite different. It keeps accusing you until you have been crushed and become useless. Remember, therefore, whenever there is a mumbling that accuses you of fault and so overwhelms you that you cannot even pray or confess or draw nigh to God, then you are definitely under Satanic accusation and must resist.

Furthermore, the results of Satanic accusation are very different from the results of the reproach of the Holy Spirit. If it is the reproach of the Holy Spirit, you will have joy, and at the very least, peace within you after you have confessed your sin. At the time you are reproved, you do suffer agony; but as soon as you confess your sin before God, you enjoy peace in your heart. Sometimes you will be filled with joy, for the heavy burden has been lifted. With Satanic accusation it is not so. Even at the time of prayer and confession, you are still bothered by his mumbling. He will insinuate that you are sinful and useless, that your confession before God is of no avail, that you will be just as weak after asking for forgiveness as you were before. These are sure signs that the accusation is of Satan; it is not the reproach of the Holy Spirit.

We should understand that the primary fields of Satanic operation are not only in the mind and in the body but also in the conscience. He tries to weaken our conscience. Be careful, then, not to fall into his snare! Do keep it well in mind that through the blood of the Lord our conscience may be purified. No sin in the world is so great that the blood cannot cleanse it. Satan, though, will attempt to weaken our conscience to such an extent that we wonder if the blood of our Lord is able to cleanse us. We feel as though we could never be forgiven. This is indeed a Satanic accusation, a lie of the devil.

Satanic accusations need never be confessed. I have found this out after many years of searching. We may wish to play it safe, and hence we confess and ask the Lord's blood to cleanse us. Let me tell you, if once you ask for the cleansing of the precious blood, then you will also have to do the same thing the second time Satan comes to bother you. And so this will go on endlessly. I have met quite a few brothers and sisters who are afflicted in just such a way as this. You can only advise them not to confess. Instead, they should say to the Lord, "Lord, pardon me for not confessing! If I actually have sinned, I still will not confess,

59

for confession carries little meaning these days. It may be Satan's accusation, so I will not even confess."

Do not be so doubleminded as to think that it is impossible for you to resist these accusations even though you wish you did not have them. If you do nothing but think from morning till night, you will be confounded. But if you resist, you will overcome. You should declare: "I resist! I do not accept these; I oppose all accusations in my conscience! I stand against these accusations which come from Satan! I stand before God under the blood, for the blood is ever efficacious for me! I deny these accusations."

Satan's accusations are many more than we imagine. If Satan cannot make you actually sin and thereby render you useless, then he will make you *feel* sinful in your conscience and thus paralyze you. He who sins becomes ineffective before God; so does he who feels sinful in his conscience. Everyone who is used of God must be free from the consciousness of sin. If such consciousness exists, a person cannot be used by God. How can one's conscience be burdened with the consciousness of sin and yet he still be used of God? So Satan always purposes to accuse us in our conscience. Hence the book of Hebrews says, "Would have had no more consciousness of sins" (10:2). This is the absolute necessity, the most basic foundation. Our conscience must not have the consciousness of sins. Yet this is the very thing which Satan seeks to bring in. As soon as there is a guilty feeling in the conscience, the whole being is weakened for all spiritual things. Remember, the consciousness of sin in the conscience does not constitute holiness. The more you are conscious of sin, the less holy you are, and also the less useful. As long as your conscience is troubled with an unforgiven sin, your effectiveness is lost.

Therefore, learn to resist all the works of Satan in your

conscience. Satan puts bad Christians out of the battle by enticing them to sin, but he gets seeking Christians out of the fight by using accusation. He disables the carnal Christian by sin and the spiritual Christian by accusation. Consequently, it is very necessary that God's children should have their eyes open to discern Satan's attack. Otherwise, they cannot walk uprightly.

4. SATAN'S ASSAULT THROUGH ENVIRONMENT

We have paid special attention these days to the matter of the discipline of the Holy Spirit.* We have noticed how the Holy Spirit so arranges all our circumstances that, even as the Word of God tells us, our hairs are all numbered (Matt. 10:30). Our hairs are not only counted as to their total number but also each is identified by its own number. God knows today when you comb your hair not only how many hairs but also which hairs have fallen!

God's ordering of our environment is clear and detailed. He has looked into all our affairs. Everything is in His hands. Yet, at the same time, Satan has asked God's permission to attack us through our environment. This is something we need to know about.

The story of Job in the Old Testament is the most prominent example. Satan was allowed not only to afflict Job's body with boils, but also to cause his house to fall, his sheep and cattle to be taken away, and his children to die. He sent down fire, wind, and enemies. All these were performed by Satan.

For another example, what did the Lord say about Peter's fall? "Behold, Satan asked to have you, that he might sift you as wheat" (Lk. 22:31). Thus we see that

* Lesson 40

61

though our environment is all arranged by God, yet many attacks may come from Satan. While the Lord Jesus was sleeping in the boat, there arose a great tempest in the sea. Peter and John were certainly not cowards. Yet, as fishermen, they judged by their experience and knew those waves would cause certain disaster. That was why they awoke the Lord Jesus, saying, "Save, Lord; we perish" (Matt. 8:25). The Lord knew, though, that on the other side of the sea in the country of the Gadarenes there were demons to be cast out and that these demons were now trying to drown Him in the sea. So, at the Lord's rebuke, the wind and the sea calmed down. Ordinarily the wind and the sea are not subject to rebuke because they do not possess personality. But here the Lord rebuked them, for Satan was behind, and Satan *is* subject to rebuke.

Whenever Satan attacks us in our environment, there are two things for us to consider. The passage we read in 1 Peter 5, referring especially to our environment, gives these two sides. It first states, "Humble yourselves therefore under the mighty hand of God" (v. 6). Then it continues with, "Whom withstand" (v. 9).

Whenever God's children encounter unreasonable attacks or causeless perils in their environment, they should on the one hand maintain before God such an attitude as, "Lord, I humble myself under Your mighty hand! I do yield to whatever You have sent me!" They must not utter any word of insubordination; instead they should learn to submit to their environment. Even if it is a Satanic attack, it nonetheless has been permitted by God and hence must be accepted. On the other hand, though, they should resist Satan by declaring, "Whatever the Lord does, I accept; but whatever Satan does, I categorically oppose. I resist everything that has befallen me through Satan!" Let me assure you, if the attack has been Satan's work, it will fade away by your resisting it.

Alas, many of God's children neither submit to the discipline of the Holy Spirit nor resist Satan's attack in their environment. This really is a problem today—no submission on the one hand, and no resistance on the other hand.

I remember an incident regarding a brother who was engaged in business. Being troubled on all sides, he accepted the difficulties as being the hand of the Lord. One day he met a servant of God on the train who asked him whether he really thought that what had happened to him looked like the Lord's doing. He answered in the negative because those things did not bear any resemblance to the working of God. Whereupon this servant of God showed him that they were the works of Satan and advised him to resist them. So the brother then prayed, "God, if these come from you, I accept; but if they come from Satan, if they are Satan's attacks, I categorically reject, I resist." He spent only a little time in prayer on the train, but by the time he returned to his own place things had wonderfully turned. The change was indeed marvelous.

Most circumstances are given us by the Lord so that we may learn lessons from them; however, there are other occurrences which come from Satanic attacks. We have no lesson to learn from them, only unnecessary suffering. The discipline of the Holy Spirit is for our spiritual building up, but Satan's attack is intended to destroy us.

How to Resist the Devil

We need, then, to learn how to resist the devil. What are the various ways of resistance?

1. Fear Not

Whenever Satan works against God's children, he must first secure some ground in them. Ephesians exhorts us, "Neither give place to the devil" (4:27). Without a foothold, Satan cannot operate. Hence, his first tempting of us will be in order to secure a ground; his next will be an assault on us from the ground he has already secured. Our victory lies in not giving him any ground from the very beginning. One very large ground, perhaps the very largest, that he seeks is fear. Satan's characteristically customary work is to instill fear in the mind of God's children, a foreboding that something is going to happen.

Let us note the words of Job: "For the thing which I fear cometh upon me, and that which I am afraid of cometh unto me" (3:25). What this verse reveals to us is of tremendous significance. Before these terrible things happened to him, Job already had had some apprehension. He was fearful lest his children would die; he was afraid that he might lose all his property. Satan's first job is to plant this fear in man. If the fear is accepted, things will soon happen; if it is rejected, nothing will come of it. Satan has to obtain one's consent before he can operate. If this consent is withheld, he cannot work, for man is created with a free will. Without man's consent, Satan can neither tempt him to sin nor attack him at will. So, in the case of Job, Satan first implanted a tiny little thought of fear in Job. Having once accepted the thought, it made Job tremble.

"Fear is Satan's calling card," said Miss Margaret E. Barber. And whenever you accept his calling card, you receive a visit from him. If you reject his calling card, you drive him away. Fear him, and he comes; fear not, and he is kept away. Therefore, refuse to be afraid! Perhaps one *will* eventually kill himself if he is obsessed by the thought of cutting his throat while shaving. How often men have thoughts of fear in them, fearful lest this or that thing happen. This is especially true of nervous people. But remember, these thoughts come from Satan and must be resisted.

To the question of what is meant by resistance, an elderly person once replied, "To resist means to say, 'Thank you, but I do not want it,' when something is offered to you." Whatever is offered you, you always answer, "No, thanks!" Though Satan may present you with this or that thing, your reaction is a simple refusal. Such an attitude is enough; it is all that is needed to defeat his purpose. Let us learn this lesson today: resist every thought of fear. Fear not, for fear will bring to you the very thing you are afraid of. May I remind you that no child of God should be fearful of Satan because Satan cannot overcome us. Although he *is* quite powerful, we have in us One who is greater than he. This is an unchangeable fact, "because greater is he that is in you than he that is in the world" (1 John 4:4). Therefore, never accept fear. He who accepts fear is a fool. Has not the Bible clearly taught that, by resisting Satan, he will flee? What place does he have in us except to retreat!

2. KNOW THE TRUTH

The second condition of resistance is to know the truth. "Ye shall know the truth, and the truth shall make you free" (John 8:32).

What is truth? Truth is the reality of a thing. When Satan tempts or frightens or attacks people, he always comes in stealthily. He never lets you know he is there. He will not proclaim aloud that he has arrived, for that would arouse your suspicion. He lies, he counterfeits. He never does anything in the light. But if you know what the reality of the thing is, it will set you free. In other words, if you know something is of Satan, you are freed. The difficulty for many children of God is their unawareness of the enemy. They may say with their mouths that it is Satan's attack, yet they do not sense it deep down in their spirits. Though their lips pronounce it to be the work of Satan, their spirits are not as clear. But the day they see the truth, really knowing that this is Satan's work, they are instantly set free.

The power of Satan lies in his deception. If he cannot deceive, he loses his power. Hence, seeing is resisting; seeing makes resistance easy. When you are surrounded with perils in your environment, you cannot overcome if you only feel that these *may* be Satanic attacks. You need to know *for sure* that these are of Satan, and then it is easy for you to withstand. To deal with Satan takes more than opposing, for it is difficult to fight against his falsehoods. But when you meet him, you need to recognize him as such; then resist, and he will flee from you.

A sister once asked me, "Satan always puts improper thoughts into my mind while I am praying. What can I do about it?" I answered, "All you need to do is to resist." But she said, "I cannot resist them away." Immediately I knew something was wrong. How could anyone say that Satan gave him many thoughts and then say that he could not resist them away? The fact must be that in spite of what she said, she did not really know that these thoughts came from Satan. So I proceeded, "Was it you who was thinking these thoughts?" After a while she replied, "I was not thinking, neither did I want to think. I wanted to pray. I could not have thought about those things." So I said, "These, then, were not your thoughts. These were instead some premeditated thoughts put into your mind." "Then really," she said, "these must have been put there by Satan." You see, formerly she had not really comprehended that these were Satanic works. Finally, I advised her to resist, and she did. She told me afterwards that the thoughts were easily withstood and they quickly faded away.

It is imperative, therefore, to recognize Satan and his works. This will make resistance easy. Failure to identify Satan renders all resistance ineffectual. By knowing Satan and his devices, half the victory is already won.

3. RESIST IN FAITH

Resistance must be done in faith. We must believe that the Lord has been manifested to destroy the work of the devil, that the blood of the Lord has overcome the attack of Satan, that the resurrection of the Lord has put Satan to shame, and that the ascension of the Lord transcends the power of Satan.

BELIEVE THE LORD HAS BEEN MANIFESTED TO DESTROY THE WORK OF THE DEVIL

The Son of God has manifested Himself! He has come to this earth! While here, He cast out every demon He met; He overcame every temptation from Satan. Indeed, "To this end was the Son of God manifested, that he might destroy the works of the devil" (1 John 3:8). Let us, then, believe that wherever the Lord Jesus goes, whenever He is manifested, the work of the devil cannot exist, for it is totally destroyed.

67

BELIEVE THE BLOOD OF THE LORD HAS OVERCOME
THE ATTACK OF SATAN

How do Christians overcome Satan? "Because of the blood of the Lamb" (Rev. 12:11). Through the death of the Lord Jesus, we are united with God into one. The primary objective of Satanic attack is to separate us from God. As long as we are one with God, Satan has absolutely no way to injure us. What, then, separates us from God? Sin alone separates us, but the blood of Jesus, God's Son, cleanses us from all our sins.

Revelation 12:11 tells us that the brethren overcame Satan because of the blood of the Lamb. With the cleansing of the blood of the Lord Jesus, we are made one with God. When we have the consciousness of sin upon our conscience, we are instantly separated from Him. As soon as the consciousness of sin comes upon us, the devil begins his attack. Without such consciousness he has no way to launch his assault. Thank God, the blood of the Lamb has overcome Satan. Today even the feeblest of God's children can overcome Satan, for every one of us has the blood.

You may not have many other things, but the blood you definitely do have. Through the blood of the Lord Jesus, you quite naturally declare that all your sins have been cleansed. Today God is your God. If God is for you, who can be against you? With your God by your side, the devil cannot attack you. The reason why he is able to accuse and attack is because he has first implanted a consciousness of sin in us. But the blood has placed you on God's side, so Satan cannot do anything with you.

Remember well that once the conscience is purified from the consciousness of sins, Satan can no longer stage his attack. The blood of the Lamb overcomes him. Is it not an amazing thing that whenever man comes before God he senses his unworthiness, but when he confronts Satan he feels guilty? Such a guilty feeling makes him susceptible to the hand of the enemy. So he needs at that moment to declare, "I am sinful; that is why you attack me. But through the blood of the Lamb I overcome you. The Lord Jesus has died for me; His blood has been shed. What can you do to me?" Let us therefore believe. Believe that the Lord was manifested to destroy the works of the devil. Believe that the Lord's death has spelled destruction to Satan's attack.

BELIEVE THE RESURRECTION OF THE LORD
HAS PUT SATAN TO SHAME

On the cross our Lord disarmed principalities and powers, making a show of them openly (Col. 2:15). Through death, He brought to nought him that had the power of death, that is, the devil (Heb. 2:14). By His death and resurrection He has utterly destroyed Satan. How did the Lord Jesus put Satan to shame? By shaking off all the works of Satan when He rose from the dead.

What is resurrection? It is a realm beyond the touch of death. Every living thing in the world is within the touch of death. Men die, animals and plants die. All living things are subject to death. There is no exception, for death has spread like a net over this entire world. It has entered into every living thing. But here is a Man who came out of death, for death could not retain Him. He has entered into a realm beyond the touch of death and this realm is called resurrection.

The life we receive at the time of new birth is this resurrection life, for the Lord regenerates us by His resurrection. This new life in us has no relationship whatever to Satan. It is absolutely beyond the reach of Satan; furthermore, it is indestructible (see Heb. 7:16 mg.). Satan did all he could at the cross, but he was completely routed and put to shame by the Lord. So we have in us a life which all the powers of Satan cannot defeat.

Always remember that Satan's attack on us can never be greater than his attack on our Lord on the cross. There he poured forth all that he had accumulated since the creation of man of wrath, cunning devices, plans, and strategy—and all for one purpose: to destroy life. But all his plans and devices were of no avail. He was defeated, and ever after he is the defeated foe. The Bible affirms that his head is bruised.

We must show brothers and sisters that there is no reason for a Christian to be afraid of Satan. By the resurrection life in us, we shall overcome. Satan is fully aware that he can do absolutely nothing to this resurrection life. His days of victory are gone! His head is broken! So his prime effort now is to prolong his days, for he has already given up the hope of victory. Resurrection life is beyond his touch. It is absolutely transcendent over the power of Satan. Therefore, let us not be afraid. Let us resist him not because he is so fierce but because this is the will of God.

BELIEVE THE ASCENSION OF THE LORD
HAS TRANSCENDED THE POWER OF SATAN

We should believe in ascension as well as in resurrection. The Bible shows us that when the Lord Jesus ascended to heaven, He was made to sit at the right hand of God the Heavenly Father, far above all rule, and authority, and power, and dominion, so that He might be

70

head over all things to the church (Eph. 1:20–22). The Lord has transcended all things and is now seated at the Father's right hand. By reading Ephesians 2 we see that we too were raised up with Him and were made to sit with Him in the heavenly places (Eph. 2:6).

Let us therefore observe this: that it is not the Lord Jesus alone whose manifestation destroys the works of the devil, whose cross and resurrection and ascension disarm Satan and his power, and who has transcended all things; all the children of God share in this transcendency of the Lord. Even the weakest members are far above all evil rule and authority and power and dominion.

The point of conflict between us and Satan lies not in the struggle to win, but rather in strife to avoid defeat. These two are vastly different. Many of God's children have a mistaken concept of war with Satan. They wrongly think that they must fight in order to win. Such an idea reveals a lack of understanding of what the gospel is. No Christian is able to fight to win. We fight because we have won. The Lord Jesus has already defeated Satan. Satan has totally lost his ground. Satan's battle today is to recover, ours is to retain. We do not fight in order to occupy; we protect what we have already occupied.

The question, then, is not victory, for Satan is already defeated. The Lord has overcome! The church has overcome! The conflict between the church and Satan is to protect the Lord's victory, not to win it. Our aim is not to wrestle victory from Satan but rather to keep victory from being robbed.

We should always triumph in the cross of our Lord. We should proclaim, "Satan, you are a defeated foe!" We must always remind him of this fact. When you resist Satan, believe this fact that he is a defeated foe. We do not

71

withstand him because of his fierceness. Not at all. I must tell you that such an understanding is a complete distortion. It will only bring in confusion. No, we stand before Satan and declare to him: "You are already defeated! You are finished. I am now in the heavenly places. I defy you and I resist you."

I hope brothers and sisters understand what is meant by resisting. Satan is a defeated foe; he is a fugitive, a prisoner who should have been totally eliminated on the cross of our Lord. Today is only the day of his escape. When the kingdom comes, he shall be completely destroyed. So today he does not tempt in open warfare; rather, he hides outside the door behind the wall to sneak in with his temptation. He does everything secretly. When that happens, do not forget that you represent the Lord God and that Satan is but a fugitive tempting you outside the wall, not inside the room. You need not be afraid of him nor resist him as though he were part of the regular army. You should announce to him, "You are completely defeated! You were done for at the cross! You ought to have been eliminated, but were not; hence your coming today is not permitted!"

The Bible states clearly that if you withstand, Satan will flee from you. He is a fugitive today, trying to deceive you at the door. You should tell him who he is; then he will run away. If you think of him as already being in your home, then you will certainly be disturbed. He comes only to deceive and to try you. If he cannot succeed, he will flee from you.

If God's children are afraid of Satan, their portion will be defeat. On the other hand, let us not deceive ourselves into thinking that Satan will not attack us. He will assault—sometimes in our thought, sometimes in our body, sometimes in our spirit, and sometimes in our environment. We will succumb to his attack only because of our foolishness. If we know our position and know that we are one with the Lord, and if we resist, he will flee from us. This resisting must be done in faith. Believe that he has fled, and he cannot but flee, for he has no ground to stand before the authority of God. We give thanks to God because He has given us the victory in Christ.

HEAD COVERING

Now I praise you that ye remember me in all things, and hold fast the traditions, even as I delivered them to you. But I would have you know, that the head of every man is Christ; and the head of the woman is the man; and the head of Christ is God. Every man praying or prophesying, having his head covered, dishonoreth his head. But every woman praying or prophesying with her head unveiled dishonoreth her head; for it is one and the same thing as if she were shaven. For if a woman is not veiled, let her also be shorn: but if it is a shame to a woman to be shorn or shaven, let her be veiled. For a man indeed ought not to have his head veiled, forasmuch as he is the image and glory of God: but the woman is the glory of the man. For the man is not of the woman; but the woman of the man: for neither was the man created for the woman; but the woman for the man: for this cause ought the woman to have a sign of authority on her head, because of the angels. Nevertheless, neither is the woman without the man, in the Lord. For as the woman is of the man, so is the man also by the woman; but all things are of God. Judge ye in yourselves: is it seemly that a woman pray unto God unveiled? Doth not even nature itself teach you, that, if a man have long hair, it is a dishonor to him? But if a woman have long hair, it is a glory to her: for her hair is

given her for a covering. But if any man seemeth to be
contentious, we have no such custom, neither the churches
of God.

1 Corinthians 11:2–16

We are going to consider now the important subject of
covering the head.

In 1 Corinthians 11:2–16, the word "brother" or "sister"
is never used. Rather, the subject, head covering, is related
to "man" or "woman." Hence, what we have here does
not touch upon our position in Christ but on God's order
in creation.

Moreover, this same passage does not assert that "I and
the Father are one" (John 10:30); it simply declares that
"the head of Christ is God" (v. 3). So the relationship here
described is not that of Father and Son, but that of God
and Christ or God and His Anointed One. It does not deal
with those things which happened in the Godhead between God the Father and God the Son. Instead, it refers
to the relationship of God with the Christ of God, Him
who was sent and anointed by God. Head covering has
nothing to do with the Godhead; it is related exclusively to
the relationship between God and His Anointed. Further,
head covering here is not considered as between Christ
and His church. It is not because Christ is the head of the
church and the church is the body of Christ that there
must be head covering. No, this is not the fact here. What
is said here is, "the head of every man is Christ" (v. 3).
Though there are many people, Christ is the head to
everyone. The headship here does not refer to the church;
rather, it shows that Christ is the head to each man. So the
relationship defined here points not to Christ and the
church, but to Christ and every man. It does not deal with

the relationships among God's children, between brothers and sisters; it does not tell what brothers and sisters in the church must do. It merely says that "the head of every man is Christ, and the head of the woman is the man." This relationship must be understood before we can know what head covering is.

God's Two Universal Systems

I would like to view this matter of head covering from far off; otherwise, it will not be easy to understand 1 Corinthians 11. To comprehend this chapter in 1 Corinthians requires that we know God and His Word. First of all we need to know that God has set up two systems in the universe: the system of grace and the system of government.

1. THE SYSTEM OF GRACE

All that concerns the church, salvation, brothers and sisters, and God's children is included in God's system of grace. Everything which pertains to the Holy Spirit and to redemption belongs to this system of grace. Within the proceedings of grace, the relationship of man and woman is such that the Syro-Phoenician woman received grace from God as much as the centurion. So did Mary as much as Peter. So, too, might Martha and Mary have been raised from the dead as well as Lazarus.

2. THE SYSTEM OF GOVERNMENT

But there is another system in the Bible which we will call the government of God. This system is entirely different from that of grace. God's government is an

77

independent system under which God does whatever pleases Him.

When God created man, He created male and female. This belongs to God's government. He created male first and female next—also a matter of His government. He does what pleases Him. He has a sovereign and independent will. When He decided that the Lord Jesus should be the seed of the woman, this too was God's government. He does not take man into His counsel.

In the garden of Eden, God gave fruit to man for food. This was God's government; He did as He pleased. After the flood, God gave the flesh of animals to men as food. It also was a governmental act.

In the beginning men spoke the same language. But then men joined together to build the tower of Babel in defiance of God. As a result, their tongues were confused so that they could no longer understand one another. This is God's governmental hand upon men. Afterward, during the time of Pentecost, God poured down His Spirit and caused people to speak in tongues. This also was the governmental hand of God.

After the tower of Babel, God scattered the people over all the earth. They became many races. This was the result of God's government. From these many races, God chose a people that dwelt alone, the race of Israel, to belong to Him—and this is grace. But to divide the people into races is government.

After a while, these many races became many kingdoms. According to Biblical history, kingdoms began later than races. First the races, and then the nations. Each kingdom had a king over its people. This also was permitted in God's governmental ordering.

During the time of the judges the Israelites were only a

race, not a kingdom. Even during Samuel's time they were still a race like other races, for they did not yet have a king to reign over them. But one day the people of Israel asked for a king, as the other nations had. In choosing this way, they brought themselves out of grace and under government. They said, "Now make us a king to judge us like all the nations" (1 Sam. 8:5). God answered them through Samuel, saying, "Now therefore hearken unto their voice: howbeit thou shalt protest solemnly unto them, and shalt show them the manner of the king that shall reign over them" (v. 9).

So, God chose Saul to be their king. As soon as Saul was chosen, God's governmental system commenced in Israel. This does not mean that God's grace no longer existed, but it does indicate that the Israelites had put themselves irrevocably under government. Thereafter they were not free to resist their anointed because he was their king. Although later on, as pertaining to grace, Saul left God, he nonetheless was still king according to government. If we trace these two different courses, we shall see two different situations. According to grace Saul failed, but according to government he still was king. Thus it was that David could not resist God's established authority.

Grace and Government Joined and Completed

These two systems of grace and government continued side by side until the coming of the Lord Jesus. Quite evidently there are two sides to God's work: the system of God's grace and the system of God's providence proceed together in the world. The priests and the prophets stand on the side of grace, maintaining the system of grace; the kings and leaders of Israel stand on the side of God's government, maintaining the system of His government.

When the Lord Jesus was on earth, on the one hand He came to be the Savior of the world, to deliver men from sin. This is according to the system of grace. On the other hand, God sent Him to the world that through the work of the cross He might establish His own authority and set up His kingdom so that the heavens might rule on the earth. This is the system of government. Its work will continue until the power of the devil is destroyed and the kingdom and the new heaven and the new earth are brought in. On that day, the two systems of grace and government will be joined into one. That is to say, that during the time of the new heavens and the new earth, these two systems will become one in the Lord Jesus. He does both sides of God's work. He works under the system of government as well as under the system of grace.

The government of God does not commence with the creation of man, but, rather, at the creation of the angels. This is quite clear in the Bible. When Satan was yet a morning star, while he was still ruling, God's governmental system had already begun. Following the creation of man, basic institutions such as marriage, husband and wife, family, and the relationship between parents and children all came within the realm of God's government.

The basic lesson that all brothers and sisters need to learn is that we should never allow grace to interfere with God's government. I say most emphatically that never in our lives should we permit grace to intervene in what God has decided in government. God wants men to respect His government, not to overthrow it. If we are ignorant of God's government, we are lawless people in the sight of God. Since we have never seen the kingdom except as it is seen in the church, it is imperative for us to see the system of government. As a matter of fact, the system of grace is for the sake of completing the system of government. The system of government is not for the system of grace, but grace is for the completion of government.

Many hold to a fundamental error: they foolishly maintain that grace can set government aside. The truth is that what God does in grace never alters God's government. The forgiveness of grace that we receive from God does not change His governmental forgiveness. No matter how much we receive forgiveness in grace, still it does not affect governmental forgiveness.

God's government is an independent principle. From beginning to end, God brings in His governmental system. Grace only complements government. The system of grace was added because of man's insubordination and rebellion under the system of government. Grace is for the purpose of redeeming and restoring those who are insubordinate and rebellious, so that they may be subject to God's governmental system. Hence, grace actually gives an assist to God's system of government.

Examples of God's Government

1. ADAM

You remember the tragic story of Adam's fall. After God created Adam, He planted a garden and put man in charge of it. God literally gave this garden to Adam and Eve. "Eden" means "pleasure." So this first couple lived in a garden of pleasure. Then they sinned against God. Even though God gave them the promise of redemption, saying that a Savior would come as the seed of the women, yet He drove them out of the Garden of Eden. It is God's grace to save, but that did not change God's government in driving out Adam and Eve.

Not only was Adam thrown out of Eden, but also God set cherubim to guard the garden so that Adam could not again enter. This too is God's government. Thus we can see that God's government and God's grace are two separate matters. Grace gives man the promise of a Savior, but God's government drives that same man out of the Garden of Eden.

2. The Israelites

Having arrived at Kadesh-Barnea, the Israelites refused to enter into Canaan; consequently, God denied them that privilege. Though they repented and then tried to enter, many of them were killed by the Canaanites, for God had barred the way. Their cries did not change God's decision (Num. 13 and 14). God has His governmental act; He will not allow men to interfere with His government.

3. Moses

Moses did not sanctify the Lord before the eyes of the people when he smote the rock twice; as a consequence he could not enter into Canaan (Num. 20:7–12). Though God had mercy on him by bringing him to the top of Pisgah, He did not allow him to enter Canaan with His people. Moses could view the land with God on Pisgah, but he could not enter in (see Deut. 34). For Moses to see the boundaries of the land of Canaan from the mountain-top was God's grace; for him not to be allowed to enter in was God's government.

4. David

After David sinned, God was gracious and merciful to him in forgiving his sin. God even gave him special grace after that incident by permitting David to have unusual fellowship with Him. Yet the sword never left his house (2 Sam. 12:7–14). This is God's government.

5. PAUL AND BARNABAS

Paul and Barnabas separated from each other because of Mark (Acts 15:37–39). Mark was Barnabas' relative (Col. 4:10). He deserted Paul and Barnabas on their first missionary trip, but Barnabas was willing to take him again on the next trip. Clearly this was due to their relationship in the flesh. After Barnabas was separated from Paul, he took Mark to Cyprus, their native place, indicating that they worked together according to the fleshly relationship. Though it may be that Barnabas was still used of God and still did a good work, nevertheless the Holy Spirit took his name out of the Bible thereafter. No doubt his name is in the book of life, but it is no longer recorded in the book of Acts. This is God's government. Under the government of God, man is not free to walk in his own way.

Submission to God's Government

So, the system of grace and the system of government are two separate matters. The humbler a person is, the more he progresses in God's governmental system. Never think that because you have entered into the system of God's grace you can therefore escape the system of God's government.

Grace can never nullify government; rather, grace enables people to obey government. May I say with all seriousness that grace gives us the strength to be subject to government. It does not make us rebellious and desirous of overthrowing government. These two systems complement each other. Grace never abolishes government. Only a fool would say that since he has received grace, he can afford to be loose and careless. What a foolish thing that would be.

The clearer a person understands grace, the better he will be as a servant or a master. The more a person knows grace, the better he is as a husband, a parent, a child, or a citizen, for he is more capable of submitting to authority. He who receives more of the grace of God knows more of how to maintain the government of God. I have yet to see one who truly knows God's grace destroy God's government.

Head Covering and God's Government

The matter of head covering belongs to God's government. For those who do not know God's government, it is impossible to exhort them to have their heads covered. They will not be able to understand how much is involved in this matter. But those who have seen God's government in God's revealed Word are able to appreciate the tremendous connection between head covering and God's government. "Now I praise you that ye remember me in all things, and hold fast the traditions, even as I delivered them to you. But I would have you know, that the head of every man is Christ; and the head of the woman is the man; and the head of Christ is God" (1 Cor. 11:2-3). What we find here concerns the government of God.

The relationship here described is not that of the Father and the Son but that of God and Christ. To use a modern expression, Christ is God's representative. The relationship between Father and Son pertains to the Godhead, but Christ sent of God touches upon God's arrangement, God's government. "And this is life eternal, that they should know thee the only true God, and him whom thou didst send, even Jesus Christ" (John 17:3). God is God, and Christ is One sent by God. This is their relationship in God's government. The Son, originally equal with God, was willing to be sent by God as the Christ. God remained on high as God, but Christ was sent down to do His work. This is the first order of events in the government of God.

In God's purpose, Christ is set up to be the head of every man; therefore, all people must obey Him. He is the firstborn of all creation and its firstfruit. He is the head of every man; every man should be in subjection to Him. This is a basic principle under God's government. Christ being the head of every man is related, not to the system of grace, but to the system of God's government. Likewise, man being the head of woman also belongs to God's governmental system. God in His government establishes man as head just as He sets up Christ as head and also Himself as head. Thus the system is completed.

God is Himself the head; He sets up Christ as head; and He further makes man to be head. These are the three great principles in God's government.

For God to be Christ's head does not touch upon the matter of who is greater; rather, it is simply an arrangement in the government of God. Likewise, under God's government Christ is the head of every man, and man is the head of woman. Such are God's arrangements; such are His appointments.

Philippians 2 is clear enough: the Lord Jesus in His eternal essence is equal with God; but in God's government He became Christ, and as Christ, God became His head. Christ Himself acknowledges in the Gospel of John that: "The Son can do nothing of himself, but what he seeth the Father doing: for what things soever he doeth, these the Son also doeth in like manner" (5:19); "For I am come down from heaven, not to do mine own will, but the will of him that sent me" (6:38); "I have many things to speak and to judge concerning you: howbeit he that sent me is true; and the things which I heard from him, these speak I unto the world" (8:26); and "I do nothing of myself, but as the Father taught me, I speak these things" (8:28). Today Christ takes His place in the government of God. According to God's counsel, He is Christ and as Christ He needs to listen to God. God the Son has no need to listen to God the Father, for God the Father and God the Son are equal in honor and glory in the Godhead. But, in God's government Christ does not stand in the place of God the Son; rather, He stands in the position of Christ, the One sent of God.

Some day the whole world will know that Christ is the head of all men, for this is God's governmental decision. Today this is known only in the church; the world has no knowledge of it. But the day will come when all the people of the world will realize that Christ is the head. He will have the preeminence in all the creation. He is the firstborn of all creation and the firstfruit. Everyone must be in subjection to the authority of Christ. Likewise, God's appointment of man as head of woman is also known only in the church today. Do you get the point? Today the church alone knows that Christ is the head of man and that man is the head of woman.

We have already seen how grace can never overthrow God's government. I trust our lesson will become clearer as we learn that grace is to support God's government, not to destroy it. How can anyone be so foolish as to attempt to use grace to interfere with God's government? The government of God is inviolable; His hand always sustains it. No one, just because he has believed in the Lord, can overthrow the Father's authority, or even undermine the authority of any government. We must not say that because we are Christians we do not need to pay taxes. No, nothing of the sort! The better Christian you are, the more you will maintain the government of God.

We are here today to maintain God's testimony in the world. God has shown us that there are three different heads: God is head, Christ is head, and man is head. This is not a matter of being brothers and sisters; it is basically a governmental arrangement. Grace is concerned with brothers and sisters, but government is different. God has sovereignly willed that the head of Christ is God Himself, so Christ must obey; the head of man is Christ, so man must obey; and the head of woman is man, and so woman should have the sign of obedience on her head.

The Meaning of Head Covering

"Every man praying or prophesying, having his head covered, dishonoreth his head. But every woman praying or prophesying with her head unveiled dishonoreth her head; for it is one and the same thing as if she were shaven" (1 Cor. 11:4–5).

The meaning of head covering is: I submit myself to God's government; I accept God's appointed position; I dare not nullify His government by the grace I have received; I do not even dare to think about it; on the contrary, I accept God's government. As Christ accepts God as His head, so should every man accept Christ as his head. Likewise, woman should representatively accept man as her head. In covering the head, the woman signifies that she is not head, that she is as if she has no head—for it is covered.

Let us remember that although in practice it is only the woman who has her head covered, yet, in reality, Christ has His head covered before God and every man has his head covered before Christ. Why, then, is it that God only requires woman to have the practice of having her head covered? This indeed is marvelous, for it involves a very deep principle.

I often feel that it is impossible to talk with some brothers and sisters about head covering because they have no knowledge of God's government. Before anyone can understand head covering, he or she must first know God's government. The whole question is settled once one sees that Christ has His head covered before God. How much more ought I to cover my head before Him! I must cover it so that it is no longer seen or exposed, for God is my head. As a matter of fact, everyone's head must be covered before God. Since Christ is my head, I cannot have my own head seen or exposed.

Here I would like to tell Christian women that God has appointed man to be woman's head. In these days when God's authority is unknown in the world, the Lord demands this order only in the church. It therefore affects the very fact of our being Christians. God requires us in the church to accept what He has appointed governmentally.

The Sisters' Responsibility

When a sister covers her head, she is standing before God on the basis of Christ's position before God and man's position before Christ. God wants the woman to cover her head in order to manifest His government on earth. This privilege falls only to woman. She does not cover her head merely for her own self; she does it representatively. For her own self, it is because she is a woman; representatively, it is because she represents man before Christ and Christ before God. So when woman covers her head before God, it is just the same as if Christ covered His head before God. Likewise, when woman covers her head before man, it is just the same as if man covered his head before Christ. Man or woman should have no head since Christ is the head. If one's head is not covered, there will be two heads. Between God and Christ one head must be covered; so too must it be between man and woman and so between Christ and every man. If one head is not covered, the result will be that there are two heads, and God's government does not allow two heads. If God is head, then Christ is not; if Christ is head, then man is not; and if man is head, then woman is not.

God calls upon the sisters to show this arrangement. It is through the sisters that God's governmental system is to be displayed. It is the sisters who are responsible to have the sign of obedience upon their heads. God specifically requires women to have their head covered when praying or prophesying. Why? Because they ought to know God's government when they come before Him. In going before God to pray for people or in going before people to prophesy for God, whether in praying or in prophesying, whether in that which goes to God or in that which comes from God, in whatever is related to God, head covering is demanded. The purpose is to manifest the government of God.

Man ought not to cover his head. It is a shame to his head if a man covers his head before woman, for the man represents Christ.

How to Cover the Head

"For if a woman is not veiled, let her also be shorn: but if it is a shame to a woman to be shorn or shaven, let her be veiled" (1 Cor. 11:6). In other words, God tells the sisters to be thorough.

No woman can keep her hair and not have her head covered. If she is not covered, she should have her hair either shorn or shaven. If she feels shameful to have her hair shorn or shaven, then she should be covered. Everything must be done thoroughly, not in half measure.

"For a man indeed ought not to have his head veiled, forasmuch as he is the image and glory of God: but the woman is the glory of the man" (v. 7). Since man represents the image and glory of God, he should not cover his head. But woman is the glory of man, so she should cover her head. If a woman does not cover her head, she cannot demonstrate that man is the head. "For the man is not of the woman; but the woman of the man: for neither was the man created for the woman; but the woman for the man" (vv. 8–9). These two verses make it very clear that the matter before us is concerned with government. "For the man is not of the woman"—this is God's doing. In God's creation man did not come by woman, but woman from the rib taken out of man. Hence, the head was Adam, not Eve. Furthermore, "neither was the man created for the woman; but the woman for the man." Just by God's ordering in creation, woman should be in submission to man.

"For this cause ought the woman to have a sign of authority on her head, because of the angels" (v. 10). The Bible does not specify what is to be used for the covering; it only states that the head, where the hair grows, should be covered. Why should the head be covered? Because of the angels.

I often am amazed at this marvelous teaching that the sisters should have on their heads the sign of authority *for the sake of the angels*. We know the tragic history of how some of the angels sinned. Satan rebelled against God. Why? Because he desired to make himself equal with God. In other words, the angel Lucifer attempted to expose his own head before God and refused to submit to His authority. In Isaiah 14, Satan constantly reiterated, "I will." "And thou saidst in thy heart, I will ascend into heaven, I will exalt my throne above the stars of God and I will sit upon the mount of the congregation, in the uttermost parts of the north; I will ascend above the heights of the clouds; I will make myself like the Most High" (vv. 13–14). Right in this passage we see an archangel falling to become Satan. Revelation 12 further shows us that when Satan fell, one-third of the angelic force fell with him (Rev. 12:4). Why did the angels fall? Because of their not being subject to the authority of God the head but trying instead to expose their own heads

Today woman has a sign of authority on her head because of the angels, that is, as a testimony to the angels. Only the sisters in the church can testify to this, for the women of the world know nothing of it. Today when the sisters have the sign of authority on their heads, they bear the testimony that, "I have covered my head so that I do not have my own head, for I do not seek to be head. My head is veiled and I have accepted man as head, and to

91

accept man as head means that I have accepted Christ as head and God as head. But some of you angels have rebelled against God." This is what is meant by "because of the angels."

I have on my head a sign of authority. I am a woman with my head covered. This is a most excellent testimony to the angels, to the fallen and to the unfallen ones. No wonder Satan persistently opposes the matter of head covering. It really puts him to shame. We are doing what he has failed to do. What God did not receive from the angels, He now has from the church. Because some of the angels do not submit themselves to the authority of God and of His Christ, the world is subject to great confusion. The fall of Satan has caused much more trouble than the fall of man. But, thank God, what He failed to get from the fallen angels, He has obtained from the church.

When many of the sisters in the church take the place given to woman and learn to cover their heads, they send out an unspoken word of testimony to the angels in the air, to the effect that God has obtained in the church what He desires. Because of this, woman must have on her head a sign of authority, a testimony to the angels.

The Extremes

People, however, may go to extremes, thinking that since the man is the head and the woman is to obey the authority of man, then woman should take the attitude of blind submission. It is a human tendency to go to extremes—to either not move a step or move to the opposite extreme. So Paul warns us with a "however," for things are not that simple. Indeed, this is the outward testimony, but what about the inward fact? "Nevertheless, neither is the woman without the man, nor the man without the woman, in the Lord" (v. 11). Why is it so? "For as the woman is of the man, so is the man also by the woman; but all things are of God" (v. 12).

In the Garden of Eden, woman was taken out of man. But after the Garden of Eden, man needs to come out of woman. No man is born without woman. As a matter of fact, man cannot do without woman nor can woman do without man. Neither can say he or she is special, for all things are of God. So the order to cover the head means no more than to have a sign of authority on the head. Since all things are of God, there is no place either for boasting or for depreciation.

"Judge ye in yourselves: is it seemly that a woman pray unto God unveiled?" (v. 13). Paul directs this question especially to the sisters. After you know that in the government of God the head of Christ is God, the head of every man is Christ, the head of woman is man, and that God has appointed woman to represent every man and also to represent Christ before God—after you know all this, is it proper for a woman to pray to God unveiled?

"Doth not even nature itself teach you, that, if a man have long hair, it is a dishonor to him?" (v. 14). Paul here uses the feeling of the church to judge this matter. "But if a woman have long hair, it is a glory to her: for her hair is given her for a covering" (v. 15). Women all over the world treasure their hair for it is their glory. They like to keep their hair. I have yet to see a woman casually throw her hair into the trash can! Hair is too precious. It seems that God gave long hair to woman for a covering. Paul explains that, since God did give long hair to woman for a covering, woman ought to add another covering onto that natural covering. Woman should voluntarily put another

93

covering over her head. This is clear if you read verses 15 and 6 together. "For if a woman is not veiled, let her also be shorn: but if it is a shame to a woman to be shorn or shaven, let her be veiled"; "But if a woman have long hair, it is a glory to her: for her hair is given her for a covering." God has covered a woman's head with hair, therefore she who accepts God's authority ought to use something to cover her hair. Otherwise she should shear the hair which God has given her. In other words, if you accept God's covering, you must add on your own. If you reject God's, then you should take off what God has given you. The Bible indicates that long hair itself is insufficient; another head covering must be added.

Today people keep neither of these two commands of the Bible. If a sister will not cover her hair but shears or shaves it, she may yet be reckoned as hearkening to the word of the Bible. But today woman neither shaves nor covers her hair—a double disobedience.

What should the obedient do? Since God has covered my head, I too will cover it. God covers me with natural hair, and I will cover it with a sign. Those who know God must add their sign to God's sign.

Regarding the Contentious

"But if any man seemeth to be contentious, we have no such custom, neither the churches of God" (v. 16). I think Paul speaks quite seriously. He well knew those Corinthians—and there are many such people, not only in Corinth of old, but in every place yet today.

"If any man seemeth to be contentious." What is he being contentious about? What is the problem that is discussed from verses 1–15, for verse 16 surely refers back to the topic of verses 1–15? Paul here is simply pointing out that it is wrong to argue against what is laid down in verses 1–15.

"If any man seemeth to be contentious." There are many who like to argue that it is not necessary for woman to have her head covered. They argue that God being Christ's head, Christ being the head of every man, and man being woman's head are matters which concern the Corinthians, not the universe. But, thank God, to be a Christian is a universal, not a Corinthian, concern. Thank God, God being the head of Christ is also a universal, not a Corinthian, affair. And I too, the least of all God's servants, say likewise: being the head of woman is a universal matter, not just a Corinthian matter.

"If any man seemeth to be contentious." Some seem to imagine that the sisters need not have their heads covered. They withstand Paul's word and oppose what he has received from the Lord and delivered to them. What does Paul reply? "We have no such custom." The "we" points to Paul and the apostles. There is no such custom among the apostles that the sisters are not covered. This is a matter which is non-negotiable. If any still wish to contend, the answer is "neither the churches of God." It is therefore beyond contention.

Paul shows us what the churches of God had decided to do. According to the custom of that time, when the Jews entered into the synagogue, they covered their heads. Both the men and the women covered their heads. They both used a veil called "tallith" to cover their heads when they went into the synagogue. Otherwise they could not get in. The Greeks of that time, however, had different customs (and Corinth, incidentally, was a Greek city). Neither men nor women covered their heads when they entered into the temples. There was no Gentile nation or race in Paul's day that required the woman to be veiled and the man unveiled. Either both men and women were veiled—as with the Jews, or no one was veiled—as with the Gentiles. Only among the Christians did the man have his head uncovered and the woman have her head covered.

So, for the man to be uncovered and the woman covered is a charge that only Christian apostles have given. It is a practice the churches of God alone hold, for it is different from both the Jewish and the Gentile customs. It is something new, and it is from God.

All the apostles believed that woman should have her head covered. If anyone today professes to be an apostle and yet does not believe in the head covering of woman, he cannot be counted as one of the apostles. He must be taken as an outsider. There is no such practice among the apostles of not believing this. If any church does not believe, Paul's answer is, "We have no such custom, neither the churches of God." None of the local churches which the apostles had visited had any such custom of arguing about woman's head covering. So the answer to any who argue is that there is no such practice as arguing about it. In verses 1–15, Paul is willing to reason, but after that he reasons no more. If any seems to be contentious, Paul says no apostle will approve of that one's opinion. If anyone wants to argue, no church will agree with his view. You are outside the fellowship of the churches as well as of the apostles.

Therefore, let our sisters cover their heads in the church when praying or prophesying. Why? To manifest that in the church God has obtained that which He has failed to get in the world, in the universe, and among the angels.

The Principle of Representation

We Christians live under two different principles: the personal and the representative. We live not only personally but also representatively before God. If I am not mistaken, in the future we shall be judged both for our own sake and in the capacity of representation.

1. ILLUSTRATED BY THE MASTERS

For example, here is a master under whom are several servants. This master is a brother in the Lord, yet he treats his servants unfairly, unrighteously, unreasonably, and harshly. In the future, he shall indeed be judged by God for his unfairness, unrighteousness, unreasonableness, and harshness. But he shall also receive an added judgment, because not only does our brother have a relationship with his servants, but also he represents our Lord as master before God. Each time he acts as a master, he represents the Lord. The way he treats his servants reflects how the Lord would treat His own. Thus, if he sins, he sins in representation as well as in personal conduct. He shall be judged for his own sins and also for the sin of misrepresenting the Lord.

2. ILLUSTRATED BY THE SERVANTS

Suppose I am a Christian servant instead of a master. If I steal, am idle, lie, cheat, or give only lip service, I will be judged for these sins. But my judgment will not stop there, for as a servant I represent all servants who serve the Lord who is in heaven. If it were only a matter of service before men, I might be able to cheat, to steal, and to be idle. Yet, whenever the Bible talks about being a servant, we are reminded that we have a Lord in heaven. So, I am not just a servant; I also represent all servants. I am a servant both as a person and as a representative.

3. ILLUSTRATED BY MOSES

Moses lost his temper in front of the people of Israel at Meribah because they tempted God. He smote the rock twice with the rod. Immediately God chided him. If, in losing his temper, Moses was wrong only as an individual even though he was also a leader of the people, he might yet be forgiven. Was it not that once before, when he saw the people of Israel worshiping the golden calf on the plain, he exhibited even greater wrath by smashing the two tables of law inscribed personally by God's hand? But God did not reprove him, for on that occasion his wrath represented God's wrath; so it was righteous. But this time when he smote the rock twice, what did God say? God said, "Because ye believed not in me, to sanctify me in the eyes of the children of Israel, therefore ye shall not bring this assembly into the land which I have given them" (Num. 20:12). In other words, Moses misrepresented God. The people of Israel thought God was angry, though in fact He was not.

Personal Position and Representative Position

Thus we see personal sin and representative sin are two different things. In reading 1 Corinthians 11:3, every sister, every woman (though you cannot find such a woman in the world) should understand that she not only has her personal position but a representative position as well. God is the head of Christ, Christ is the head of every man, and man is the head of woman. For this reason, woman should have her head covered.

In having her head veiled while praying or prophesying, the sister proclaims before God that no one in the whole world should expose his head before Christ. Indeed, no one should expose his head before God, nor should anyone have his own opinion or idea before Christ. In the presence of Christ, all heads must be covered, all our opinions and judgments must be denied. Let us confess to the Lord, "You are my head." As a sister, your head is covered because you are in a representative position. Indeed, you represent the whole universe. You declare to the world what everyone should do before Christ.

Head covering in itself is a small matter, but it constitutes a very great testimony.

THE WAY OF THE CHURCH

In Revelation chapters 2 and 3, we have seven churches. At the time John wrote the book of Revelation these seven churches were local churches in Asia Minor. There were many local churches in Asia Minor, but out of these many God especially chose seven. His declared purpose in so doing was to use them as prophetic churches, for Revelation 1:3 definitely states that this is a prophecy. By choosing these seven churches as prophetic churches, God prophesies to us the way the church will go on earth.

Why must we particularly study Revelation 2 and 3? There is a deep, important reason for it. In these chapters God intends to show us what the church will experience in the two thousand years since Revelation was written, and what kind of church He condemns and what kind He approves. It is therefore imperative for us to understand these two chapters. With a right understanding of them we will be able to know the way the church takes. We will know how to please the Lord by being the right kind of people in the right kind of church. Otherwise, we cannot be good Christians.

The First Church—Ephesus

To the angel of the church in Ephesus write: These things saith he that holdeth the seven stars in his right hand, he that walketh in the midst of the seven golden candlesticks: I know thy works, and thy toil and patience, and that thou canst not bear evil men, and didst try them that call themselves apostles, and they are not, and didst find them false; and thou hast patience and didst bear for my name's sake, and hast not grown weary. But I have this against thee, that thou didst leave thy first love. Remember therefore whence thou art fallen, and repent and do the first works; or else I come to thee, and will move thy candlestick out of its place, except thou repent. But this thou hast, that thou hatest the works of the Nicolaitans which I also hate. He that hath an ear, let him hear what the Spirit saith to the churches. To him that overcometh, to him will I give to eat of the tree of life, which is in the Paradise of God.

Revelation 2:1–7

The first church is Ephesus, representing the church at the end of the first century at the time of the writing of the book of Revelation. The situation of the church at that time was like that of Ephesus.

The Second Church—Smyrna

And to the angel of the church in Smyrna write: These things saith the first and the last, who was dead, and lived again: I know thy tribulation, and thy poverty (but thou art rich), and the blasphemy of them that say they are Jews, and they are not, but are of the synagogue of Satan. Fear not the things which thou art about to suffer: behold, the devil is about to cast some of you into prison, that ye may be tried; and ye shall have tribulation ten days. Be thou faithful unto death, and I will give thee the crown of life. He that hath an ear, let him hear what the Spirit saith

to the churches. He that overcometh shall not be hurt of
the second death.

Revelation 2:8–11

The second church is Smyrna which stands for the
church after the death of John, from the second century to
the beginning of the fourth century. During this period,
the church was persecuted by the Roman Empire ten
times. So Smyrna describes the condition of the church
under persecution from the post-apostolic period until the
time Constantine accepted Christianity.

The Third Church—Pergamum

And to the church in Pergamum write: These things saith
he that hath the sharp two-edged sword: I know where
thou dwellest, even where Satan's throne is; and thou
holdest fast my name, and didst not deny my faith, even in
the days of Antipas my witness, my faithful one, who was
killed among you, where Satan dwelleth. But I have a few
things against thee, because thou hast there some that hold
the teaching of Balaam, who taught Balak to cast a
stumblingblock before the children of Israel, to eat things
sacrificed to idols, and to commit fornication. So hast thou
also some that hold the teaching of the Nicolaitans in like
manner. Repent therefore; or else I come to thee quickly,
and I will make war against them with the sword of my
mouth. He that hath an ear, let him hear what the Spirit
saith to the churches. To him that overcometh, to him will
I give of the hidden manna, and I will give him a white
stone, and upon the stone a new name written, which no
one knoweth but he that receiveth it.

Revelation 2:12–17

The third church is the church in Pergamum. At the
beginning of the fourth century, that is, in the year of our

Lord three hundred and thirteen when Constantine accepted Christianity as the state religion, the church entered into the period of Pergamum. The word "Pergamum" means "marriage," for during that period the church and the world were married and thus united together. Formerly the world persecuted the church; now the world welcomed the church. Thus, with the world coming into the church, the nature of the church was drastically changed. In Greek, *gamos* means "marriage." The English word "polygamy" comes from the Greek root *gamos*. "Pergamos" means "Behold, now is the marriage."

Of the seven churches, the first three have already passed away, but the last four continue on. When the first church passed away, the second came; with the fading of the second the third was introduced; and the ending of the third ushered in the fourth. But the fourth did not pass away when the fifth was born; the fourth and the fifth continued on together. And the sixth continued on with the fourth and fifth, and the seventh with them too. So, when the seventh church came, the fourth, the fifth, and the sixth churches still existed. Thus the seven churches in Revelation 2 and 3 are divided into two parts: the first three that have already passed away, and the last four that remain until the second coming of the Lord Jesus.

If this is so, the prophecies concerning Thyatira, Sardis, Philadelphia, and Laodicea will all have words indicating that they continue till the coming of the Lord. Thus, to Thyatira: "Nevertheless that which ye have, hold fast till I come" (2:25); to Sardis: "Remember therefore how thou hast received and didst hear; and keep it, and repent. If therefore thou shalt not watch, I will come as a thief, and thou shalt not know what hour I will come upon thee" (3:3); to Philadelphia: "I come quickly: hold fast that

which thou hast, that no one take thy crown" (3:11); and
to the last church, Laodicea: "He that overcometh, I will
give to him to sit down with me in my throne, as I also
overcame, and sat down with my Father in his throne"
(3:21). Being the last one, naturally Laodicea continues
until the second coming of the Lord Jesus. Thus the first
three churches (Ephesus, Smyrna, and Pergamum) do not
have the promise of the Lord's coming that the last four
have. This seems to indicate that the last four will
continue on until the second coming of the Lord Jesus.

In order to know our way as children of God, we need to
consider carefully the last four churches. Since there are
four different kinds of churches on earth now, all of which
will continue up to the second coming of the Lord Jesus,
what should we do? What relationship should a child of
God have to these churches? We need to choose carefully
from these four lest we stay in a church that the Lord has
condemned. If we do that, we will suffer great loss before
the Lord. We have merely touched upon the first three in
this lesson, for they have all passed away. Now we want to
look closely at the last four.

The Fourth Church—Thyatira

And to the angel of the church in Thyatira write: These
things saith the Son of God, who hath his eyes like a flame
of fire, and his feet are like unto burnished brass: I know
thy works, and thy love and faith and ministry and
patience, and that thy last works are more than the first.
But I have this against thee, that thou sufferest the woman
Jezebel, who calleth herself a prophetess; and she teacheth
and seduceth my servants to commit fornication, and to eat
things sacrificed to idols. And I gave her time that she
should repent; and she willeth not to repent of her

fornication. Behold, I cast her into a bed, and them that commit adultery with her into great tribulation, except they repent of her works. And I will kill her children with death; and all the churches shall know that I am he that searcheth the reins and hearts: and I will give unto each one of you according to your works. But to you I say, to the rest that are in Thyatira, as many as have not this teaching, who know not the deep things of Satan, as they are wont to say; I cast upon you none other burden. Nevertheless that which ye have, hold fast till I come. And he that overcometh, and he that keepeth my works unto the end to him will I give authority over the nations: and he shall rule them with a rod of iron, as the vessels of the potter are broken to shivers; as I also have received of my Father: and I will give him the morning star. He that hath an ear, let him hear what the Spirit saith to the churches.

Revelation 2:18–29

The fourth church is Thyatira. After the Roman Caesar accepted Christianity as the state religion, it was supported by political power. In the past, political power had been employed to suppress Christianity; now it was used to support Christianity. It became a promoter. As a consequence, Christianity was not only married to the world, but was also exalted by the world. The word, "Thyatira," in the Greek means "high tower." She had now become a high tower, visible to, and respected and worshiped by, the world.

Those who study the Bible agree that the church in Thyatira points to the Roman Catholic Church, for in that system the church and the world are joined together. Consequently, the church has gained quite a position in the world. What trouble does that cause? It produces a prophetess by the name of Jezebel who teaches God's servants. The church comes under her rule and is controlled by her. The problem in the Roman Catholic Church is similar to that described by the fourth parable of Matthew 13 in which a woman hid leaven in three measures of flour. The Bible uses this woman to signify the Roman Catholic Church.

What about this woman? "But I have this against thee, that thou sufferest the woman Jezebel, who calleth herself a prophetess; and she teacheth and seduceth my servants to commit fornication, and to eat things sacrificed to idols" (2:20). The two principal sins of Jezebel are fornication and idolatry. Sinners in both these areas are subject to excommunication. The Lord condemns the teaching of Jezebel.

"And I gave her time that she should repent; and she willeth not to repent of her fornication. Behold, I cast her into a bed, and them that commit adultery with her into great tribulation, except they repent of her works" (vv. 21–22). The church in Thyatira followed the teaching of Jezebel. Fornication means confusion. When men are in confusion, they are considered as having committed adultery. Here we see the confusion caused by the mixture of the Roman Catholic Church with the world.

All religions throughout the world have their own special goddesses. The Buddhists have their goddess; the Greeks worshiped Aphrodite, and the Romans worshiped her under the name of Venus. But no one could find a goddess in Christianity. So, they made the Virgin Mary the goddess in Christianity. Though the name used is Mary, the reality is the Greek and Roman goddess. This is fornication, for it is confusion.

Many of the Romans believed and worshiped the sun. They set apart December 25th of each year as the birthday of the sun. They chose that date because

December 22nd is the shortest day of the year, the winter solstice. After that, the days begin to lengthen and the nights shorten. So these sun-worshipers made December 25th the birthday of the sun. It was their time for a big festival. Many of those who accepted Christianity could not stand to see their heathen friends celebrate so jubilantly while they themselves had nothing to celebrate. So they conceived the idea of transforming December 25th into the birthday of the Lord, since, they claimed, the Lord Jesus was the true sun. Thus today we have Christmas on that date. According to its name, Christmas belongs to Christianity; in fact, though, it is a day which belongs to the religion of sun-worship. Let us note that this is fornication, confusion, in the sight of God.

The church is the temple of God. In the Old Testament time, God's temple was built either of wood or of stone. But in the New Testament days, we find God allowed that old temple to be destroyed till no stone was left upon another stone. Today the temple of God is the believers: "Know ye not that your body is a temple of the Holy Spirit?" (1 Cor. 6:19). This, then, is true Christianity. But the Roman Catholic Church of today has built immense buildings. The Greeks were famous for their artistic constructions, and the Romans, who succeeded the Greeks, were also very skillful architects. All their gods had temples. Only the Christians did not have a temple for people to visit. So these Roman Christians departed from the teaching of the apostles and erected huge buildings. Perhaps no other construction in the world can surpass the Christian cathedrals in majesty and grandeur. These cathedrals are called the temples of God. Whether it be the cathedral in Milan or St. Peter's Cathedral in Rome or Notre Dame Cathedral in Paris, they are all immense buildings. But let us remember, this idea originated from the heathen religions. The idea of heathen temples was transferred to Christian temples. Again, according to its name it is Christian, but in fact it is from heathenism. Christianity has committed spiritual fornication with the heathens.

Moreover, in the Biblical New Covenant all of God's children are priests. All those who believe in the Lord Jesus are priests unto God, thus all serve God. But the Roman Catholic Church was attracted to the priesthood in Judaism as an intermediary class—on the one side there are God's people, and on the other side there are God's ordained priests. So they carried the Old Testament Jewish idea of priesthood into the church and divided the Roman believers into two distinct classes. One class wears priestly robes and puts on priestly mitres. They wear the same things as the priests of the Old Testament, except that they have added many other things to their adornment. They not only copied Judaism, they also absorbed things from the Greek and Roman religions. In doing these things, they have changed God's order. This is fornication, for according to the Bible fornication is confusion.

Furthermore, the Roman Catholic Church has borrowed many Old Testament articles of worship—such as candles, candlesticks, and censors—for their own use. They added these to the other things brought in from heathen religions. If this is not fornication, what is it? They adopted heathen things, things pertaining to idol-worship, superstitious things, things which the Romans called mystery, and then they named them Christian. This is fornication, impurity. It is not Christianity but great confusion.

The Lord reprimands the Thyatira church not only for fornication but also for idol-worship. Is it not strange that God should reprove the church for idol-worship? Yet the fact remains that the church was worshiping idols. In the Old Testament days, people worshiped the brazen serpent. In the Roman Catholic Church, they worship the crucifix. They tell people that they have found the cross, and out of that wood they make many small crosses. They literally worship the crucifix.

The Lord Jesus is God, and God has no form; but they make an image to worship. They make images of Mary, of Peter, of Mark. They fill the earth with images! Naturally the appearance of the image depends on the level of culture. The higher the culture, the better looking their images. Roman Catholic churches now are full of idols! When Catholics pray, they do not pray to God in heaven; instead they light candles before the images, and cross themselves with the sign of the cross. They make images of the Father, the Lord Jesus, Mary, Paul, and Peter. Even the martyrs of past centuries have had images made of them. If a person dies and is canonized to be a saint, his image will be made. These images are prayed to by the people.

Relics of martyrs have also become the objects of their homage. It may be the leg of a martyr or a single bone buried under the altar, but they begin to worship the relic. If you are familiar with the Roman Catholic Church, you know how it is filled with idols.

The church in Thyatira represents the Roman Catholic Church. It is a church system condemned by God. Therefore, the word of the Lord to those in the Roman Catholic Church is, "Come forth, my people, out of her, that ye have no fellowship with her sins, and that ye receive not of her plagues" (Rev. 18:4).

According to Revelation 2 and 3, Thyatira is the fourth church. It succeeds Pergamum. Ephesus has passed away, Smyrna has passed away, and Pergamum has passed away. But after Thyatira comes, it does not pass away. It continues till the coming again of the Lord Jesus. We who believe in God and are God's children should try our best not to touch the things in the Roman Catholic system. Do not touch those unclean things, lest you be affected. I remember Mr. D. M. Panton once said that though their books are so full of errors, you may not sense them as you read. Since there are so many errors, it is rather difficult for you to distinguish error from truth. You are only confused. Therefore, let us not follow the Roman Catholic Church.

The Fifth Church—Sardis

And to the angel of the church in Sardis write: These things saith he that hath the seven Spirits of God, and the seven stars: I know thy works, that thou hast a name that thou livest, and thou art dead. Be thou watchful, and establish the things that remain, which were ready to die: for I have found no works of thine perfected before my God. Remember therefore how thou hast received and didst hear; and keep it, and repent. If therefore thou shalt not watch, I will come as a thief, and thou shalt not know what hour I will come upon thee. But thou hast a few names in Sardis that did not defile their garments: and they shall walk with me in white; for they are worthy. He that overcometh shall thus be arrayed in white garments; and I will in no wise blot his name out of the book of life, and I will confess his name before my Father, and before his angels. He that hath an ear, let him hear what the Spirit saith to the churches.

Revelation 3:1–6

111

The fifth church is Sardis. This church represents the restored church or the remnant church, that which remains. It succeeds Thyatira, though Thyatira does not cease to exist. It therefore succeeds but does not substitute Thyatira.

What is the condition of Sardis? Verses 1–4 show us that the characteristic of Sardis is that it has a name that it lives and yet is dead.

Sardis represents the Protestant church. The Protestant church follows the Roman Catholic Church. Though the Reformation is included in Sardis, yet it does not represent the Reformation. It represents the Protestant church.

The Roman Catholic Church not only became powerful, it also became despotic and cruel. Consequently, the nations of Europe could no longer stand its oppression and started a movement toward reformation. During the time of the Reformation, two different forces evolved; one was of God and the other was of man.

What was of God is seen in Martin Luther. Though but one man, he stood against the pope, the cardinals, the priests, and the entire Roman Catholic Church. During that period, God gave men two things: an open Bible, and the truth of the justification by faith. In various places those who loved the Lord rose up to undertake the work of reform. They gave their lives to seal the truth to which they testified. Though they were oppressed and harassed by Rome, yet they believed the Lord would do the work of restoration. So they sacrificed everything to undertake the task of reformation. The Holy Spirit worked mightily in those days encouraging people to be faithful in the service of the Lord and to understand the Bible as He gave light. The number of the saved was greatly increased. They declared that they were saved not by their own works nor by the priests but by depending on God. This truly was a mighty work of the Holy Spirit!

Meanwhile, there were many politicians who opposed Rome. They made use of the Reformation to satisfy their political aspirations. Thus the Reformation movement was complicated and became a political reform as well as a religious reform. This was also due to the fact that the Roman Catholic Church was not only a religious power but also a political power. Its rule extended over all Europe. What was originally a religious reform took on an overtone of political reform when kings and rulers and politicians of many countries seized this opportunity to free themselves from the Roman yoke and become free nations. Formerly both their churches and their governments were controlled by Rome; now both were set free.

For this reason, Protestantism became a movement which combined the forces of the church and the world to overturn Rome. It was not just the church opposing Thyatira; political forces also were against Thyatira. Consequently, the so-called national churches came into being: in Germany the Lutheran, in Sweden also the Lutheran, in England the Anglican, in Holland the Dutch Reformed—all of these national churches developed.

At the beginning, many of God's people came out of the Roman Catholic Church for the sole purpose of leaving the fornication and idolatry of Rome. But later other people stepped in to help God's people; even political powers wanted to help make it easier. The Christians rather naively accepted the help of political powers, but this influenced them to copy Rome in some aspects when they began to establish new churches. Even as Rome was a church in which politics and religion were mingled, so the churches which Protestantism produced also became a mixture of politics and religion. This is an undeniable fact of history.

The Roman Church managed political affairs as well as spiritual affairs. For instance, if the believers in Germany had wanted to return to the New Testament after they had left Rome, they would have seen that the church—that is, God's people—was a poor and defenseless body on earth. But due to the inadequacy of their light plus the involvement of political helps, Germany set up its own national church, the German Church, independent of Rome. The term, "German Church," was to imply that all Germans were included in the church. The English did the same thing by setting up the Anglican Church. Anyone who was born an Englishman could ask the Anglican priest to baptize him. According to the rule of a national church, the scope of the church is as comprehensive as that of the nation. It is not just that all believers are in the church, but that all citizens of that country may be baptized into the church. This is how the Protestant church got the name in Revelation that it lives, and yet is actually dead.

This is characteristic of Sardis, that it has a name that it lives and yet is dead. That which marks the Protestant church is a continuous commingling of the world and the church. Formerly, Rome ruled over the entire world; now each nation has its own church. There is, therefore, a great mixture of God's people with unbelievers. Such is the situation of the Protestant church.

This, however, has not prevented the presence of many spiritual leaders in the Protestant church, for there actually have been a number of men used of God. Hence the Lord says: "But thou hast a few names in Sardis that did not defile their garments: and they shall walk with me in white; for they are worthy." This too is a special feature of the Protestant church. Spiritual giants have been raised up continuously, but these are individuals, not a corporate body.

The early history of the Protestant church is basically that of the records of the national churches, but its latter history is filled with records of dissenting churches. In the national churches, people came into the church through baptism, instead of by faith. Church membership was the result of baptism, not of faith. Later on, many felt that national churches were not Scriptural because it is by faith that one becomes a child of God. And so dissenting churches developed.

Other believers may have seen some new truth or even emphasized a certain truth. Since the national church was more concerned with maintaining its institution than with serving God, naturally God raised up people here and there who discovered a certain truth or who condemned a certain sin. These people would organize independent churches, the so-called dissenting churches. Many of these people passed through severe persecution and opposition. The stories of John Bunyan, the persecution of the Presbyterian Church in Scotland, the migration of the Puritans to the New World, and the opposition to the Methodists, especially John Wesley and George Whitefield, are all well-known.

When they were first separated from the national churches, these people were accused of being divisive. Being dissenters, they were called sectarian. In actuality, though, it was not they who created the division but the national churches, for it was the national churches who included too many (the unbelievers) in them. God's children ought to follow the Lord's Word and come out from among them.

Let us therefore see that oneness is not condoning sin but, rather, condemning sin. We are told by people today that in order to be one we have to bear with sin, for if we all learn to bear, then we will be one. Indeed, in the national churches a great number of things are not of God. If a person's conscience is touched by the Holy Spirit and he begins to be aware and reject certain sins, then he will be labeled by those who do not reject such sin as divisive. As a matter of fact, the real problem is not with him—for he sees—but with those who do not see.

If God's children were all to judge sin, they would be united as one. The oneness of God's children is not something carnal, but spiritual; it is a oneness with the Lord. If we do not judge sin, we may become one, but we are not one with the Lord.

In the history of the Protestant church, God has constantly raised up now and then one or two to whom He reveals His thoughts, His judgment of certain things. Those who do not or will not see often accuse those who see and obey God as being divisive. Yet, if all God's children today would judge sin and deal with things which are not of God, they would all be one with the Lord and one with each other. Therefore, judging errors and condemning sin is the true foundation of oneness.

There is another feature in the history of the Protestant church. The first thing God does is to raise up a man. Through the grace that man receives, great blessing is brought in. The first generation really has many glorious days. During the second generation the situation may not change much. But toward the end of the second generation, people may begin to think of how to preserve God's grace in their midst. They may conclude that they must organize in order to keep this grace. So, by the end of the second generation, organization comes in. Sometimes this organization may begin as early as at the close of the first generation; sometimes it may be as late as the third generation.

These Christians can believe God to give grace, but they cannot believe Him to keep the grace. They believe God to bestow blessing, but they do not believe Him to continue to bless. As a consequence, they devise human creeds, rules, and methods to maintain the blessing they have received. But if God's fountain is shut, the pool can only become drier, it cannot rise higher. So, in the third generation, their condition is quite dead, as dead as the church which they had originally left. Thereafter, God has to lay hold of another person or persons to whom He can give new revelation, new blessing, new separation, and new grace. This time will again become a time of revival. Again, the first generation may be full of blessing, the second generation begin to organize, and the third generation begin to decline. Thus is the history of the Protestant church.

Formerly people left the national churches and set up new churches. Now other people are forced to leave these new churches. When people left the national churches, it was because they had become dead; now people have to leave these new churches because they too have become dead! The entire history of the Protestant church is characterized by a living name but a dead body. Protestantism lives persistently on the border between life and death. There is living as well as dying. It is not completely dead because there are yet a few names who have not been defiled, who are especially used by God. These are the giants in the Protestant church. They are worthy to walk with the Lord in white.

Both Sardis and Thyatira, the Protestant church as well as the Roman Catholic Church, were reprimanded by the Lord. What, then, is the way for believers?

The Sixth Church—Philadelphia

And to the angel of the church in Philadelphia write: These things saith he that is holy, he that is true, he that hath the key of David, he that openeth and none shall shut, and that shutteth and none openeth: I know thy works (behold, I have set before thee a door opened, which none can shut), and thou hast a little power, and didst keep my word, and didst not deny my name. Behold, I give of the synagogue of Satan, of them that say they are Jews, and they are not, but do lie; behold, I will make them to come and worship before thy feet, and to know that I have loved thee. Because thou didst keep the word of my patience, I also will keep thee from the hour of trial, that hour which is to come upon the whole world, to try them that dwell upon the earth. I come quickly: hold fast that which thou hast, that no one take thy crown. He that overcometh, I will make him a pillar in the temple of my God, and he shall go out thence no more: and I will write upon him the name of my God, and the name of the city of my God, the new Jerusalem, which cometh down out of heaven from my God, and mine own new name. He that hath an ear, let him hear what the Spirit saith to the churches.

Revelation 3:7–13

Here we have the sixth church, the church of Philadelphia. "Phileo" means "to love," and "adelphos" means "brother." Philadelphia is brotherly love.

Of the seven churches, only two churches escape reproof and of those two, only one, Philadelphia, is wholly approved and praised. For Philadelphia alone, there is praise without reproof.

What is the characteristic of Philadelphia? "I know thy works (behold, I have set before thee a door opened, which none can shut), and thou hast a little power, and didst keep my word, and didst not deny my name" (Rev. 3:8). That which characterizes Sardis is a struggling with death. Because the church in Sardis was mingled with the world, it needed to struggle for life and to start out anew all the time. But Philadelphia is brotherly love. Here there is a return to the love of the brethren. It is no longer the world, because everyone is a brother. It has no need to struggle free from death and the things of death that tend to cling on. Philadelphia is simply a restoring to the original position of the brethren before God where all is love.

As Sardis came out of Thyatira, so Philadelphia comes out of Sardis. The Protestant church comes out of the Roman Catholic Church, while Philadelphia comes out of the Protestant church. We cannot point out which group is the so-called Philadelphia, but it is quite evident that it is a new move of the Holy Spirit. This new move lifts people out of dead Sardis and places them in the position of love of the brethren—in other words, the position of the body where the only recognized fellowship is that of love. This is Philadelphia.

Philadelphia possesses two special features: one, they keep the Word of the Lord and, two, they do not deny His name. Here is a group of people who are led by God to learn how to keep the Lord's Word. God opens His Word to them so that they can understand. There is no creed in their midst, only the Word of God. There is no doctrine, only the Word. There is no tradition, only the Word. There is no opportunity for man's opinion, only the Word of God. After the apostles, this is the first church which the Lord praises, for now a group of people has completely returned to the Lord's Word. To them no authority other than the Lord's, no teaching, no creed is of any use.

It is possible for people to be able to preach and understand doctrine and yet not know the Bible. It is possible to learn a creed and accept it without knowing the Word of God. Does this sound somewhat strange? If the church needed a creed, the Lord would have given it to us. Today, people analyze the Bible and form it into a creed. The Bible is infinite in nature, but the creed is definite. The Bible is involved, but the creed is simple. A creed can be understood by the foolish, but the complexities of the Bible are intelligent only to a certain group of people, for it requires a certain condition to understand it. The Word of God is wide open for those with life to enter in; but a creed is something so widely opened that all who desire to may come in. The Bible cannot be understood unless the reader has life and singleness of eye before the Lord, but a creed can be understood by anyone who has a clear mind as soon as it is read.

People may think the way is too narrow; so they try to widen it in order to get people in. But the Philadelphians reject all creeds; they simply return to the Word of God. "Thou didst keep my word," says the Lord. In all of church history, only in the era of Philadelphia has the Word of God been so much understood. Only in Philadelphia does God's Word have its rightful place. In other times, people accepted creeds and traditions, but the church in Philadelphia accepts nothing but the Word of God. They walk according to God's Word. Throughout church history, there have never been so many ministers of God's Word as in Philadelphia.

"Thou didst not deny my name," says the Lord. This, too, is a special feature of Philadelphia. After such a long history of the church, the name of the Lord Jesus has unexpectedly become the very last name. People pay more attention to men's names—perhaps to Peter's or the other apostles. Or Christians may choose to call themselves by some other preference of theirs such as doctrine or nationality. Many take pride in saying, "I am a Lutheran," or, "I am a Wesleyan"—the names of men. Many proudly declare themselves to be Coptic or Anglican—named after a place or a country. These many names completely divide God's children! It looks as if the one name, the name of the Lord Jesus, is not sufficient to separate us from the world.

If anyone should ask you, "Who are you?" and you answer, "I am a Christian," he will not be satisfied. He will insist upon knowing what kind of a Christian you are. I remember when I was abroad, I was once asked who I was. I said, "I am a Christian." The person replied, "That is meaningless."

The Lord Himself considers His name to be quite sufficient for His children. But only in Philadelphia is His name reckoned as sufficient. There is no need for many names, for names separate. His name is enough! Remember, the Lord is quite concerned about this matter.

Many brothers ask me the question, "What do the overcomers in Philadelphia overcome?" Do you realize the difficulty here? The overcomers in Ephesus naturally have overcome the tendency to forsake first love; the overcomers in Smyrna have overcome the external threat of death; the overcomers in Pergamum have overcome the bondage and the temptation of the world; the overcomers in Thyatira have overcome the teaching of the woman; the overcomers in Sardis have overcome spiritual death; and the overcomers in Laodicea are to overcome the condition of lukewarmness and the deceit of pride. But what do the overcomers in Philadelphia need to overcome? Since the Lord is pleased with all they have done (of the seven letters, this is the only letter which shows the Lord's complete acceptance), what else do they need to overcome? Everything has been accepted, everything is fine. Philadelphia is a church after the Lord's own heart. Yet in this church, the Lord still gives promises to the overcomers. What must they overcome? It seems there is nothing that needs especially to be overcome, for there seems to be no problem.

However, the Lord does give His warning here. "I come quickly: hold fast that which thou hast, that no one take thy crown" (Rev. 3:11). This is the only warning in the letter to the Philadelphians. The Philadelphians must be careful to hold fast what they have. In this they must overcome. In other words, they must not lose that which they already have. Do not change it or alter it. Keep what you have and do not drop it. This is the one warning to Philadelphia. The Lord has only one request: keep that which you have. You have not done anything wrong, but you must keep on doing what you have already done. You have sensed the blessing of God in what you did. Now you should keep on in the same way.

The problem with Philadelphia is that if they do not keep what they have, God will raise up other people to take away their crown. Originally the crown was given to them, but if they depart from their position, their crown will be taken by others. What the Philadelphians must overcome is that they must not lose what they already have possessed. This is quite different from the other seven churches. Let us therefore take note of the Lord's Word. Only one church, the church in Philadelphia, is after the Lord's own heart. Its characteristics are that it keeps the Lord's Word and it does not deny His name. May we never be negligent in these matters.

The Seventh Church—Laodicea

And to the angel of the church in Laodicea write: These things saith the Amen, the faithful and true witness, the beginning of the creation of God: I know thy works, that thou art neither cold nor hot: I would thou wert cold or hot: So because thou art lukewarm, and neither hot nor cold, I will spew thee out of my mouth. Because thou sayest, I am rich, and have gotten riches, and have need of nothing; and knowest not that thou art the wretched one and miserable and poor and blind and naked: I counsel thee to buy of me gold refined by fire, that thou mayest become rich; and white garments, that thou mayest clothe thyself, and that the shame of thy nakedness be not made manifest; and eyesalve to anoint thine eyes, that thou mayest see. As many as I love, I reprove and chasten: be zealous therefore, and repent. Behold, I stand at the door and knock: if any man hear my voice and open the door, I will come in to him, and will sup with him, and he with me. He that overcometh, I will give to him to sit down with me in my throne, as I also overcame, and sat down with my Father in his throne. He that hath an ear, let him hear what the Spirit saith to the churches.

Revelation 3:14–22

Of the seven churches, five are reprimanded, one is without reproach (Smyrna), and one is wholly approved. The church which is wholly approved is Philadelphia. The Roman Catholic Church, the Protestant church, and Philadelphia all continue till the second coming of the

Lord Jesus. The seventh one, Laodicea, also continues to the Lord's coming again. If Sardis comes out of Thyatira, and Philadelphia comes out of Sardis, then Laodicea comes out of Philadelphia. Do you see that one begets the other?

The problem now is: if Philadelphia should fail, it will become Laodicea. Do not think Laodicea is the Protestant church, for this is represented by Sardis. The Protestant church today can only be Sardis; it can never be Laodicea. It takes the fall of Philadelphia to become Laodicea. Sardis is an improvement over Thyatira. It comes out of Thyatira and is an advancement. Philadelphia comes out of Sardis and is also an advancement. Laodicea comes out of Philadelphia, but it is a regression. All these four churches continue on until the second coming of the Lord Jesus.

Laodicea is a mutilated or distorted Philadelphia. Once brotherly love is lost, then immediately people's rights and opinions take over. This is the meaning of the word "Laodicea." It was the name of a city, named by a Roman prince after his wife whose name was Laodios. The prince changed the name into Laodicea, which in Greek means, "the people's rights or opinions."

When Philadelphia falls, the emphasis becomes more on "people" than on "brethren," more on "people's rights" than on "brotherly love." Love turns to rights or opinions. When brotherly love is a living thing, people's rights are a dead thing; but whenever brotherly love is waning (and the body relationship with its fellowship in life will be fading too), people's opinions begin to prevail. The Lord's mind is not sought; things are settled by the majority opinion. Philadelphia has fallen into Laodicea.

"I know thy works, that thou art neither cold nor hot: I

would thou wert cold or hot" (Rev. 3:15). This is the character of Laodicea. "Because thou sayest, I am rich, and have gotten riches, and have need of nothing; and knowest not that thou art the wretched one and miserable and poor and blind and naked" (v. 17). This is what Laodicea is. Though it is neither hot nor cold, it is full of spiritual pride before the Lord. To say, "I am rich," ought to be enough, but Laodicea emphasizes it with, "and have gotten riches"; then this is further reinforced by, "and have need of nothing"! But the Lord sees differently, for He replies, "thou art the wretched one and miserable and poor and blind and naked." From where does this spiritual pride come? Undoubtedly it is based on the past history. Once the Laodiceans were rich; so now they imagine they are still rich. Once the Lord showed mercy to them; now they remember that past history, though they are no longer in touch with the reality of it.

In the Protestant church today, one rarely meets anyone who boasts of his spiritual richness. I have met many leaders in the Protestant church both in China and abroad. Their consensus is: we fall short, we are not what we ought to be. I have yet to meet a proud man in Sardis. But those who were formerly of Philadelphia, those who once kept the Word of God and did not deny His name but who now have lost the abundant life, they are the ones who boast. They remember their past history, though they have lost their past life. They remember how they grew rich and lacked nothing; but they are now poor and blind. Let me tell you, only fallen Philadelphia, the Philadelphia which has lost its life and power, can boast of its riches.

Therefore, brothers and sisters, if we desire to continue on the course of Philadelphia, we must learn to be humble before God. Sometimes I have heard brothers say, "The blessing of God is in our midst." I acknowledge the truth of it, yet I feel we need to exercise extreme caution in saying this, lest inadvertently it exudes a Laodicean flavor. If one day we incline to say that we are rich and have grown rich and have need of nothing, we are very close to Laodicea.

Remember, there is nothing which is not received. Even if the people surrounding you are all poor, you still need not know that you are rich. Those who live before the Lord are not conscious of their wealth. They who come forth from the presence of the Lord are rich, yet they are not aware of their riches. May God be merciful to us that we may learn to so live before the Lord that, being rich, we know not our riches. It is better for Moses not to know the radiancy of his countenance, for, once known, it may become Laodicea. If it is known, it may end up in lukewarmness. Those of Laodicea know everything, but nothing is real before God. If we profess to have everything yet nothing can induce us to give up our life, if we remember our past glory but forget our present condition before God, then the past was indeed Philadelphia, but alas, the present is surely Laodicea.

The Way of the Church—Our Choice

Today I hold before you these four churches. The Roman Catholic Church, the Protestant church, Philadelphia, and Laodicea will all continue till the coming again of the Lord Jesus. Consequently, every child of God must choose today the way of the church for him. Do I want to be a Roman Catholic or do I choose to be a Protestant? Will I follow the external unity of the Roman Catholic Church or will I follow the many denominations of the Protestant church? Or would I rather walk in the way of

Philadelphia? Or was I once of Philadelphia but am now living in the past glory and boasting in my past history just as the Laodiceans do? Please remember: If people commence to be proud before God and yet depart from life, neglecting reality while remembering the past history of glory, they will soon fall into a condition of the people's rights and opinions. They sound democratic but they have no body relationship. How can they know brotherly love if they do not know the bondage of the body, the authority of the body, and the life of the body?

Since all these four churches continue on, we must choose to remain faithfully in Philadelphia. Do not be curious about the Roman Catholic Church. Curiosity often leads to disaster. Do not touch the many sects in the Protestant church, for this is not God's way. The Bible shows us clearly that, though the entire Protestant movement is blessed of God, it nevertheless has many things the Lord condemns and reprimands.

We should learn to stand in the position of Philadelphia. Keep the word of the Lord and do not deny His name. Stand on the ground of brethren, not of names. Do not be proud. Do not boast before the Roman Catholic Church. Do not boast before the Protestant church. Do not boast before the many sects and denominations. The moment you are proud, you become Laodicea. You are no longer Philadelphia. Brothers and sisters, which way are you traveling? May God give grace to His children that all may walk in the straight path of the church.

The way of the church as appointed by the Lord is Philadelphia. The Lord's way for us is only one—Philadelphia. Walk in it. Be careful lest there is pride. The greatest temptation to the Philadelphian way is pride: "I am better than you! My truth is clearer and broader than yours! I have only the Lord's name—I am not like you who have another name!" Pride will plunge us into Laodicea. Those who follow the Lord have nothing of which to be proud. The Lord will spew out the proud. May the Lord be merciful. I warn you not to utter arrogant words! Live in the presence of God and refrain from saying any boastful words. By living constantly in God's presence, we will not see our riches. Therefore, we will not be proud.

ONENESS

The subject before us is Christian oneness. We have already seen how the body of Christ is to be manifested on earth. Does not Paul tell the Corinthian believers, "For as the body is one, and hath many members, and all the members of the body, being many, are one body; so also is Christ" (1 Cor. 12:12)? Paul does not say, "so also are Christ and His people." He merely asserts, "so also is Christ." In other words, the head is Christ, the body is Christ, the members are Christ.

When Paul met the light near Damascus, he was challenged with, "Saul, Saul, why persecutest thou me?" In reply to his question, "Who art thou, Lord?" the Lord said, "I am Jesus whom thou persecutest" (see Acts 9:3-5). But the "I," Jesus, is in heaven. How can an earthly person, Paul, with a letter from the high priest, persecute Jesus of Nazareth who sits at the Father's right hand? Here we see the oneness of the body of Christ—the head, the body, and the members are all Christ. This is the reason our Lord did not say to Saul, "Why do you persecute My people?" or "Why do you persecute My church?" Instead He said, "Why do you persecute Me?" Here we can see that Christ and the church are one.

Oneness Is on the Earth Today

The Christ whom Saul persecuted was manifest on earth, for He could be—and was being—persecuted. "So also is Christ"—the body of Christ is also on earth. The body is one; yet the members are many. Though there are many members, the body is only one. It is on earth, for it is subject to persecution. Saul persecuted what he could find of that body on earth, but the Lord remonstrated with him that he was persecuting Him.

This matter is of the greatest significance. The body of Christ is one. As a person has only one body, so the oneness of the body of Christ should be manifested on earth now. It should not wait to be demonstrated in heaven. In 1 Corinthians 12 it says of the body of Christ that, "Whether one member suffereth, all the members suffer with it; or one member is honored, all the members rejoice with it" (v. 26). This distinctly shows that the body of Christ is something on earth. If it were in heaven, we might speak of honor but we could not talk about suffering, for it is impossible for the body to suffer when in heaven. Only on earth is a member open to suffering; only on earth is the body subject to persecution. For this reason, the oneness of the body of Christ is not just a future reality in heaven but is also a present fact on earth.

In His prayer in John 17, the Lord Jesus prays for the oneness of the church on earth: "That they may all be one; even as thou, Father, art in me, and I in thee, that they also may be in us: that the world may believe that thou didst send me" (v. 21). If we omit the middle parenthetical section of this passage and read the remainder: "That they may all be one, that the world may believe that thou didst send me," we can clearly see that the oneness of the church is to induce the world to believe. Since those who are to believe are people in the world, it is evident that this oneness must be manifested before the world. The Lord expects the world to believe. This oneness, then, is present on earth today.

So the first problem to be solved is the manifestation of Christian oneness on earth today; we are not only to wait expectantly for it in heaven at a future day. Naturally, all Christians will be one in the future in heaven, but today this oneness must be practiced and thus manifested on earth. Those who have already become believers should not comfort new believers by saying, "You need not be concerned now with the oneness of the church or of the Christians. One day in heaven we will all be one." No, what the Lord demands today is oneness on earth. The responsibility for it is upon us all. Therefore, do not postpone this to the future in heaven. To have this Christian oneness manifested on earth now is a matter of the very first order.

Oneness Is Limited to the Body

Many people try to be one with everyone who professes outwardly to be a Christian, disregarding whether such ones are really God's people and have new life, disregarding whether they really are members of the body of Christ. The oneness these people advocate exceeds the scope of the body of Christ. Their oneness includes those who are spiritually dead, and this is something foreign to the body of Christ. Such oneness is not permitted by God's Word, for what the Bible promotes is the oneness of the body.

I would like to stress here that the oneness of the body is the unity of the church. The church's unity is limited to the body and cannot be extended beyond the body. The Word of God never sanctions oneness with nominal Christians.

1. TARES AND WHEAT

Sometimes people quote Matthew 13 on the subject of oneness. The second parable says:

> "The kingdom of heaven is likened unto a man that sowed good seed in his field: but while men slept, his enemy came and sowed tares also among the wheat, and went away. But when the blade sprang up and brought forth fruit, then appeared the tares also. . . . And the servants say unto him, Wilt thou then that we go and gather them up? But he saith, Nay; lest haply while ye gather up the tares, ye root up the wheat with them. Let both grow together until the harvest: and in the time of the harvest I will say to the reapers, Gather up first the tares, and bind them in bundles to burn them; but gather the wheat into my barn" (vv. 24–30).

Many people misconstrue the oneness of the body to be the oneness of the wheat and the tares. They think oneness is not only with the wheat but with the tares as well. They do not realize that the Lord is not dealing with the question of oneness in this parable. He is not advocating the mingling of believers and unbelievers. He only suggests here that believers should not try to kill or harm unbelievers. The Roman Catholic system has erred in trying to weed out the tares—those whom they call heretics. They err not only in principle but also in practice. In weeding out the tares, they also pull out the wheat, for they consider Protestants as heretics.

The Lord does not charge us to weed the tares out from the world. He does, however, teach us that in the church there must be separation. Letting these two grow together till the time of harvest refers not to wheat and tares in the church but in the world. The field in the parable is the world, not the church (Matt. 13:38). In other words, we are not required to remove nominal Christians from the world, as the Roman Catholic system has attempted to do. Nominal Christians should be allowed to live in the world, but this by no means implies that oneness of the body of Christ includes them.

Nowadays in the so-called Christian organizations, there are great multitudes of unbelievers. These societies receive unbelievers, the tares, into their churches. The Lord, though, only permits tares in the world; He does not allow them to be received into the church. He wants Christian oneness to be maintained in the church though not in the world.

There are two extremes today: those like the Roman Catholic system who do not allow the tares to exist in the world but prefer to weed them out, and those like the societies which permit unbelievers to remain in the church. In the national churches, as long as one is a national of the country and is born of nationals, he is given baptism and is received into the church. This opens the door of the church to unbelievers. Such action is unscriptural.

Even John Wesley in drafting *The Discipline of the Methodist Church* inserted, "All who wish to escape the wrath to come may become Methodists." This statement, however, is too general. Wesley was one greatly used by God; he far surpasses us in many things. But still we may protest to him, "Brother, this statement of yours is too general." Buddhists, too, must be numbered among those who desire to escape the wrath to come, but the church

133

does not include them. So, the church cannot include all who merely seek escape from the wrath to come.

Let us see now what the church is. The church is composed of all who have the life of Christ, all those to whom Christ has imparted Himself. These people are the body of Christ. Consequently, Christian oneness includes all the children of God. It does not embrace any nominal Christian who has not been regenerated and still belongs to the world. Such people do not belong to the church and thus are not included in its oneness.

2. A MATTER OF PRINCIPLE

A servant of the Lord once told me, "We do not reject any saved person!" "Assuredly," I agreed, "we do not expect any church to reject saved people. But may I ask you if you reject those who are not saved?" He retorted, "You are too serious, for you presume to know who is saved and who is not. We don't do that." I acknowledged that his challenge was reasonable, but still I remonstrated, "I do not ask if you know who is saved and who is not saved. What I ask is, suppose you know that a certain person is not saved, will you still receive him into the church? The controversy is not over fact but over principle. If you know one is unsaved, will you receive him?" "I am afraid we have to receive him even if we know he is not saved," he honestly conceded. If a church receives an unsaved person in principle, it cannot be reckoned as a church. To receive an unsaved person in principle is different from receiving him in fact. In fact, we do not know whether Simon the Sorcerer in Acts 8 was saved or not. Indeed, many under questioning seem to be saved, but in fact they may not be saved. Nevertheless, they are examined as to their faith, for to do so is a matter of principle. If any society is willing to receive people without attempting to find out whether they are or are not saved, that society has breached the principle of the oneness of the body of Christ.

The question today is not one of procedure but one of principle. For example: It has been ruled that all descendants of Huang-ti may become Chinese citizens. This is a principle. If a person belonging to the Ta-Ho race (the Japanese) is erroneously accepted as a Chinese, this is an error in procedure. But if it is ruled that the Ta-Ho race may also be considered as Chinese, then the principle is changed. Through the centuries, many mistakes in the matter of who is Chinese have been made. We too have often made mistakes as to who is saved. May God be merciful to us, for we have nothing of which to be proud. Nonetheless, it is clear that the Lord has ruled in principle that the church should not open its doors to receive unbelievers.

So, brethren, if any group holds an open door policy in principle, if it welcomes unbelievers as well as believers, it definitely is not a church. It is the world, because only in the world do the tares and the wheat grow together. The church is the gathering of the called-out ones. How can it accommodate both the called and the uncalled?

If a group or society opens its door wide enough to receive unbelievers as well as believers, it is not a Christian group and its oneness is not a Christian oneness. Some day the Lord will open my eyes to see that I must leave this group. When I do so, I do not break Christian oneness, for such a group does not have Christian oneness. It is a mixture, a confusion. The command of God is that we come out of such confusion.

"Be not unequally yoked with unbelievers: for what

fellowship have righteousness and iniquity? or what communion hath light with darkness? And what concord hath Christ with Belial? or what portion hath a believer with an unbeliever? And what agreement hath a temple of God with idols? for we are a temple of the living God" (2 Cor. 6:14-16a). You should know who you are. You are a temple of the living God. Therefore, you have nothing to do with idols. "Even as God said, I will dwell in them, and walk in them; and I will be their God, and they shall be my people" (v. 16b). You are a temple of the living God in whom He dwells and with whom He walks. He is your God, and you are His people.

What, then, is the issue? "Wherefore come ye out from them, and be ye separate, saith the Lord, and touch no unclean thing; and I will receive you, and will be to you a Father, and ye shall be to me sons and daughters, saith the Lord Almighty" (vv. 17-18). Here we are shown that we must come out from any association which bears the name of being Christian and yet includes both believers and unbelievers.

It is imperative that the church should not receive unbelievers in principle. Once a brother asked me, "Did you ever receive people erroneously?" Though at that time I was not conscious of having done so, yet I answered, "Maybe, but very few." "What is the difference, then, between you and us?" he questioned. My reply was, "If any unbeliever desires to come among us, he has to come in by night and climb over the wall. With you, he can come in at twelve o'clock noon and enter by the opened gate." Let us never be so arrogant as to think we are infallible. By mistake we may baptize the wrong people and receive them, but they have to sneak in, for this is not according to our principle. We do not say that we have absolutely no error in our procedure. Of course, we do seek to be very careful before God so as not to make mistakes. But whoever errs purposely, whoever adopts an erroneous principle, cannot be recognized as a church.

The children of God have no obligation to keep oneness with such a group. Because it is not Christian oneness, we need not keep it. We are only obliged to keep the oneness of the wheat, not the oneness of the wheat and the tares. There are many so-called church groups today which contain both believers and unbelievers. They desire to preserve an outward appearance of unity. We know very well that such unity is not worth preserving, for it will only undercut the real oneness of the body.

Oneness Includes All the Body

The scope of Christian oneness is very precisely defined. It includes all children of God. The measure of the body of Christ is the measure of Christian oneness. Christian fellowship is as comprehensive as the body of Christ.

We wish to draw the attention of all brothers and sisters to this thing: God wishes His children to be one in the Holy Spirit. God does not say that just any oneness will do; He insists that oneness must be in the Holy Spirit. Only this is called Christian oneness. It is a oneness in Christ. To keep Christian oneness, we must keep in Christ, in the body, in the oneness of the Holy Spirit. So, the scope of Christian oneness is as inclusive as the body.

1. DIVISION

Today there is much misunderstanding about oneness. Many mistakenly assume that as long as there is oneness, it satisfies God's desire. But if the oneness is not circumscribed by the body of Christ, it is not worth keeping. To keep a oneness which is smaller than the body of Christ is to make what Scripture calls division. God wants us to keep the oneness of the Holy Spirit and the scope of that is the body of Christ.

Some Christians believe that baptism should be by immersion. This is true to the Bible; it certainly has no error. However, such Christians sometimes adopt a rule that they will not receive anyone who is not immersed, even if he is a child of God and belongs to God. Thus they make a teaching the basis for their oneness. This is not the oneness of the Holy Spirit because it creates a group smaller than the body.

Suppose a brother has been with this group for sometime. He has, indeed, had very good spiritual fellowship there and he has received much spiritual help. But one day God opens this brother's eyes. He sees that although they are all God's children, their group cannot be recognized as a church because they receive only those who are immersed. They reject those of God's children who are not baptized by immersion. Having been enlightened, he leaves the group.

After a while, another brother exhorts him, saying, "We are all Christians, we are all God's children, we are all brothers. God commands us in His Word to love one another. So you should not leave us. If you leave us, you sin against Christian oneness. If you leave, you divide God's people; you become sectarian." Having heard this, the first brother takes up his Bible and reads and rereads the New Testament. He finds that God's children must, indeed, be one. So he concludes that he must not leave.

Brethren, do you detect anything wrong with his conclusion? The error therein is quite evident. When people insist that there should be no division, we need to first know what a division is. Division means to divide the body or to divide from the body. 1 Corinthians 12 speaks of schism in the body; it refers only to division in the body, not to division in any group other than the body, for any group other than the body is in itself a division. The Christian oneness which God prescribes is as comprehensive as the body of Christ. We should never sin against it, nor can we ever come out of it. But should a group smaller and narrower than the body of Christ demand oneness, we affirm that this is not Christian oneness. It is not the unity of the Holy Spirit. Why? Because this oneness is not as comprehensive as the oneness of the body. New believers should realize that they do not violate or destroy Christian oneness if the group or organization they leave is smaller than the body.

2. FORSAKE DIVISION

Let us proceed further: whatever group is less in scope than the body of Christ must not be preserved. To the contrary, we need to come out of its oneness, for any child of God who attempts to keep a oneness which is smaller than the body of Christ infringes upon the true oneness of Christ.

There were strifes in the church at Corinth, for some said they were of Paul; others, of Apollos; others, of Cephas; and still others, of Christ. Paul reacted most violently against those who spoke like that. He remonstrated with them, saying, "Was Paul crucified for you? or were you baptised into the name of Paul? . . . Whereas there is among you jealousy and strife, are ye not carnal?" (1 Cor. 1:11–13; 3:3).

Suppose there were in Corinth some brothers by the

names of Mark, Stephen, and Philip. One day Philip stood up and said, "We all feel that God's servant, Paul, has been used by God in a special way, and that we should pay more attention to his teaching. We have heard him preach, we have read his letters, and we have all been much helped. Indeed, our fellowship in the Lord is most sweet. Recently, however, I sense that we have not been doing the right thing, for there are hundreds of believers in Corinth today, and we are only a few dozen. We ought to gather with those others and fellowship with them."

Suppose, then, that Mark and Stephen and the rest of the brethren stood up and refuted Philip, saying, "This is sin! When the Lord Jesus was on earth, He prayed to the Father that we might be one. The Lord Jesus wants us to be one, and yet you are thinking of going away. You intend to go a different way. You are not one with us. You do not glorify the Lord! If you are not one with us, how can the world see that we are one and thus believe in the Lord? You sin if you go out from our midst. You are sectarian."

Brethren, what is this? Is it not the very thing that many are trying to say today? They themselves are already divided, for they declare, "I am of Paul; and I of Apollos; and I of Cephas; and I of Christ." And yet they exhort those who wish to go out from them to keep Christian oneness. But their oneness is not as comprehensive as the body of Christ; theirs is only as large as those who belong to Paul. To keep a oneness which is smaller than the body of Christ is itself a division. The mere stating that I am of Paul is divisive in spirit.

May God open our eyes to see that the body of Christ is one and that sects are divisions. In 1934, there were already one thousand five hundred well organized denominations. All these sects called themselves churches. In fact, though, they all have narrowed the scope of the body of Christ. Today many brothers and sisters would like to return to the full scope of the body so as to have the fellowship of the body, but they are accused of destroying oneness. But they have not destroyed the oneness of the body. Only as the oneness of sects is eliminated can there be a return to the comprehensive oneness.

Christian oneness is as inclusive as the body of Christ. It nonetheless excludes all that which is not of the body. Any oneness which is smaller than the body cannot be reckoned as Christian oneness. The more we keep man-made oneness, the more sectarian we become. We need to come out of these smaller onenesses before we can enter into the comprehensive oneness. We must forsake the small oneness in order to get into the all-inclusive one. Never fancy that oneness alone is sufficient; the question to be asked is, "What kind of oneness is it?" Not every oneness counts; it has to be the oneness of the body. Anything that is smaller than the oneness of the body is unacceptable to Christians, for it is a division and God repudiates it.

3. Meaning of "Sect"

The Greek word "hairesis," translated "sect," "party," or "heresy" is used nine times in the Bible; six times in Acts where it invariably is translated as "sect"—such as the sect of the Sadducees, the sect of the Pharisees, or the sect of the Nazarenes (Acts 5:17; 15:5; 24:5, 14; 26:5; 28:22)—and three times in the epistles. Let us look more closely into the three occasions in the epistles.

First, "For there must be also factions (hairesis) among you, that they that are approved may be made manifest among you" (1 Cor. 11:19). When the Corinthian believ-

141

ers gathered together, there were divisions or factions. What is a faction? It is something that can only be found in a church. In Corinth there was a church. All these believers belonged to the church at Corinth. But the day came when some of the believers said they were of Paul, others of Apollos, others of Cephas, and others of Christ. Not only was their tone bad, but also their attitudes were improper. Strifes and jealousies were rampant, while the love of Christ was absent. When they met, they gathered in parties. This is sectarianism.

An accusation of being sectarian can only be made in the church. Outside the church, no such accusation is possible, for such a sin cannot be committed elsewhere. For instance, a person can only commit the sin of rebellion against a legitimate government; if there is no legal government, one cannot commit the crime of rebellion. When one individual and the legitimate government are at odds, it constitutes rebellion; but when there is no legal government, one cannot be reckoned as rebellious. Likewise, sectarianism can only be committed within the church. It is disapproved by God.

Second, "Now the works of the flesh are manifest which are these . . . wrath, factions, divisions, parties (hairesis)" (Gal. 5:19-20). What is a sect or a party? It is a work of the flesh. Paul speaks to us as well as to the Galatians and the Corinthians when he says that sectarianism is not only unspiritual but also carnal. He makes a list of the works of the flesh in which he mentions fornication, uncleanness, lasciviousness, idolatry, sorcery, enmities, strifes, jealousies —and also parties or sects.

The answer as to whether a Christian may be permitted to commit fornication would invariably be no. The answer to whether a Christian may worship idols again would definitely be no. But the answer to whether a Christian may divide into sects would probably be that though there is outward division, yet in the heart there is no such division. This sounds like the idol-worshipers who tell us that, although they worship outwardly, their hearts are not in it. Let me tell you, such actions are inexcusable. They are condemned by God.

It surprises me to find people who profess to be God's servants and yet in their writings affirm that it is quite proper for Christians to remain in sects. What if a servant of God were to write a book condoning Christian worship of idols? What if he were to write justifying Christian fornication, lasciviousness, jealousy, or wrath? No doubt you would judge that such a person is not a servant of God. But when someone writes that Christians may be divided into sects, why do you not judge as the Lord judged? Please remember, we have no liberty to choose from among the works of the flesh. Sects are as manifestly the works of the flesh as idolatry, fornication, wrath, and sorcery. They are all inscribed in that condemned list.

The word "hairesis" has a distinct meaning in Greek, but in English it is translated "factions" in 1 Corinthians 11:19, and "parties" or "heresies" in Galatians 5:20. All who know English know that "heresies" is just a translation of the Greek word "hairesis." It does not give any clear sense unless it is traced to its original Greek. In the original, it means sects; it is condemned by God as a work of the flesh. Consequently, we are not obliged to keep the oneness of a sect. As a matter of fact, to keep such a oneness is to destroy Christian oneness.

Third, "But there arose false prophets also among the people, as among you also there shall be false teachers, who shall privily bring in destructive heresies, denying

143

even the Master that bought them, bringing upon themselves swift destruction" (2 Pet. 2:1). Know, therefore, that sects or heresies are destructive, being brought in by false teachers. All who belong to God ought to learn how to maintain Christian oneness. We must not try to maintain any oneness which is smaller than the body.

Oneness Is Not Association

Once people see the destructiveness of sects and God's condemnation of them, they begin to realize the need for Christian oneness. They become conscious of the inappropriateness of having fellowship with any group smaller than the body of Christ and, at the same time, they become aware of the need to have fellowship with all the children of God. In this day, such an awakening is quite extensive among Christians. Some time ago, a Christian leader wrote me a letter in which he stated, "Although we do not approve of the teaching against sects, we nevertheless agree that Christian oneness is a must." Indeed, Christian leaders today do know they should stress Christian oneness rather than sectarian unity.

I acknowledge that over the past few decades many have stressed oneness. Nonetheless, the fruit of this has not been the oneness of the body but the oneness of association. This latter type of oneness is a human production. It is what is called the ecumenical movement or an interdenominational work. I personally feel this is a midway expediency; it falls short of either end.

Let me be very frank: if sects are right, they should be positively maintained; if they are wrong, they should be cast away. Instead of this, what do people do? Some acknowledge that sects are wrong, yet they retain them;

144

others assert that they are right, yet they reject them. Such double-mindedness toward sects is certainly an unchristian attitude. Since we know that the Lord wishes His children to have the fellowship of the body, we ought to cast aside everything but the fellowship of the body of Christ.

Most to be feared are those who adopt a midway expediency. They readily admit that sects are wrong and yet they do not have the heart to reject them. Instead, they want to reform the sects. They acknowledge that denominations are unscriptural; yet they try to organize an association of denominations. They do not know where they stand. A Christian should not be double-minded. It should be yea, yea or nay, nay. Any compromise or accommodation must be rejected.

The scope of oneness, as we have mentioned, should neither be greater than the body—allowing the tares to be included, nor smaller than the body—dividing into sects or special groups. But those who adopt a midway expediency bring in another possibility: the scope of oneness may be as big as the body of Christ; yet, within it, there may be many separated squares, like a checkerboard. This is an association, not a union, not oneness.

Were it necessary that the church have sects, God would certainly have proposed it in His Word. But the Bible only tells us that the church is a body and the body is one, with all the members closely knit. Where is the ground for an association of sects in the Word of God?

The Bible affirms that the body is made of members. In other words, the member is the unit of the body. Today, those who sponsor associations see the body of Christ, and yet they are not willing to pay the price for having the fellowship of the body. Though they indeed emphasize the body of Christ, the unit they adopt is not that of members but rather of groups or sects. But the unit of Christian fellowship is the Christian; the body is made up of all the Christians. We fellowship with one another because we are all believers. To organize believers into groups and then unite these groups together for fellowship adds something extra to what God has ordained.

God has joined all His children in the body of Christ so that He may manifest His glory. But men attempt to unite different sects—groups that have already formed different opinions, ways, and teachings—into one big association. They first divide according to man's idea and then unite according to God's thought. They seem to be able to please both God and men. They preserve fleshly sects while arriving at Christian oneness. This is the mentality behind the formation of associations. We emphatically protest that this is nothing other than giving ground to the flesh. The Lord has shown us clearly that parties or sects are the works of the flesh.

Once the body has been divided into sects, it cannot be made into the body again by putting these sects together. To do that makes an association, not the body. Can you cut a man into pieces and then form him again by putting the pieces back together? No, the life is gone. Likewise, it is foolish and absurd to cut the body of Christ into hundreds of sects and then unite them together. You do not have the body, only an association. May we realize before God that we must not divide the body of Christ into many sects. This we know: united there is the body, divided there are the members; between the body and the members there is no intermediary organization. The ecumenical movement today will not give us the body of Christ. It does give us a gigantic association, a human organization—the product of a guilty conscience.

Oneness Needs to Be Maintained

How, then, should we maintain oneness? We have to reject any organization which includes unbelievers, for it is not a church. We must leave all sects, for they divide the body of Christ. And we should repudiate all associations of sects, for this is a work of the flesh.

If there is to be a church in a locality, its scope must be as comprehensive as the body of Christ: it must include all God's children in that locality—nothing more, nothing less. Whether the people of God are willing to take this stand or not is their own responsibility. But those who wish to follow the Lord must be faithful. They must take this non-sectarian ground. The basic rule of the church is that the church neither includes any unbelievers nor allows any sort of association to substitute for the body. We stand on the ground of the body of Christ, for this is the scope of the church. And this is the one and only course God's children must take everywhere.

God has put us on this pure ground of oneness on which all children of God must meet. What if some do not gather together? We dare not make any false claim; we only maintain that we do stand on the ground of the body of Christ.

Without hesitation, we concede that there are many brothers and sisters in the sects, in national churches, and in various associations. If they are faithful to the Lord, they ought to return home and stand with us on this body ground. The door is always open to them. But, as for us, we cannot but stand on body ground.

Some people insinuate that the church of God has been dissolved and its door closed because so many of God's children have wandered into various denominations. We, however, by our stand declare that the children of God on earth are not scattered and the door of the church cannot be shut. We are doing our best to maintain this testimony. We have a home in which our Father, our Lord, and the Holy Spirit dwell jointly with us. However few we may be, is not the presence of the triune God sufficient?

Yet, could we boast that we have a home if we were unaware of losing those brethren who stray outside? What kind of a home would we have? Something would be drastically wrong. No, to us it is sad and heartbreaking if there is a single brother or sister left wandering in the sects. There are two attitudes we must hold: on the one hand our attitude is to keep and maintain the ground of the oneness of the body; on the other hand it is to be humble, never arrogant. While standing on the ground of oneness, we cannot be so proud and satisfied because we are at home. Remember, there are yet many roaming abroad who belong to this home. Let us be humble and learn to pray. Let the door be ever opened to them. Let us expect them to come home, whether they come to stay or only temporarily. The ground of the home must be maintained. Do not err so seriously as to surmise that there is no church today.

The Basis of Oneness Is Judgment

Finally, let brothers and sisters remember one thing: the oneness of the body is not only a oneness of Christians but it is also a oneness with God.

In the Old Testament, we can see that each time God is present there will be judgment. The presence of God is the presence of the law, and consequently it is also the presence of judgment. God is holy. If He were not present, judgment would not be brought in. But to keep the oneness of the Christians, we must maintain the presence of God. God's presence brings in law and judgment. As soon as something is not right, God judges it. Without God's presence, everything can be tolerated; with God's presence, no sin can be left unjudged. If a church tolerates sin, it can never keep the oneness.

1. FORSAKE SIN

May brothers and sisters see what the basis of oneness is. It is very elementary: oneness is based on the forsaking of sin. God's children today are so divided because of many sins. Where there is sin and evil, there is bound to be separation. It is a fundamental mistake to assume that patience or forbearance is the basis of oneness. No, the Bible never advocates either patience or forbearance as the basis of oneness. It rather affirms that oneness is based on the forsaking of sin.

If anyone wishes to fellowship with God, he needs to walk in the light. If we walk in the light as God is in the light, we have fellowship with one another (1 John 1:7). So we may say that fellowship is the basis of oneness, and fellowship is based on dealing with and forsaking sin. If we are all in God's light, we have fellowship one with another; otherwise, we have no way to fellowship.

"Wherefore come ye out from among them, and be ye separate, saith the Lord . . . and I will receive you, and will be to you a Father, and ye shall be to me sons and daughters, saith the Lord Almighty" (2 Cor. 6:17–18). God bases His fellowship with us on our coming out and being separated. Do not, for the sake of gaining man's affection, ever lose fellowship with God. This is the cause of many defeats.

2. PAY THE PRICE

In order to become a vessel of honor before God, one needs to purge himself from the vessel of dishonor. Let everyone who names the name of the Lord depart from unrighteousness. If a man purges himself, he will be a vessel of honor. As a vessel of honor, he is able to follow after righteousness, faith, honor, and peace with them that call on the Lord out of a pure heart. Those who drew their swords and were determined in their hearts to stand on God's side and slay their own brethren were alone qualified to be Levites (see Ex. 32:25–29).

A price must be paid to maintain the scope of oneness. Do not imagine that oneness may be obtained by having more love or greater forbearance. There is no such possibility, for the basis of oneness is the forsaking of sin. Everything which sins against the oneness of Christians must be cast off. Christians today are not one, yet not because their love is inadequate, but because their sins are not fully dealt with. There is no lack of human patience and affection today, but what does it avail?

God has opened the eyes of some today to see the body and the scope of the church. Once they have been caught up with the oneness of Christians and have disentangled themselves from the bondage of human affection, they naturally are free to go forth and follow the Lord. Do not blame these who have come out; rather, blame your own lack of singleness of heart, your own disinclination to go forth. They see because they are willing to forsake sin and unrighteousness, willing to depart from the dishonorable, willing to deny their natural affection, and ready to stand on the ground of the body. They are not trying to surround you with human affection; neither do they preach oneness to you. Today if you too are willing to pay the price of forsaking unrighteousness and of sacrificing man's love and affection, you also shall see the body of Christ and will naturally be one with them.

3. OBEY GOD

How much unrighteousness and how many sins and offences have been committed against the body of Christ! Let me tell you, if a person is faithful and obedient to the Lord, he may be one with all who love the Lord. But if he desires to maintain another kind of oneness, he will be contaminated by the same kind of sin and unrighteousness which others have.

Many complain that those who go out lack forbearance, love, and patience. The fact is that those who do not go forth are actually those who lack patience and love and obedience. It is not that the hearts of those who come out are too hardened, but that the hearts of those who remain behind are less determined.

If all brothers and sisters rose up to judge sin, the fellowship among Christians would be one. If all obeyed God, they would see what the oneness of the body is. Flesh, sects, and divisions would naturally be cast off, and God's children would all be one.

So, the basis of oneness is not in tolerating sin but in judging sin. There is no possibility of oneness between those who judge and those who do not judge. If anyone desires to seek oneness with God's children, he must judge sin with all the children of God. If some judge sin and others do not, can there be oneness? But it is right to judge sin. He who judges sin is one with all who judge sin. May God be merciful to him who does not judge sin that he too may rise up and judge. Oneness is possible only outside organizations, methods, sects, and associations. The body of Christ alone is the scope of the oneness of God's children.

LOVE THE BRETHREN

We know that we have passed out of death into life, because we love the brethren. He that loveth not abideth in death.

1 John 3:14

Of the four gospels, the gospel of John was the last written; of all the epistles, the epistles of John were the last written; and of all the books of the Bible, the book of Revelation was the last written. In other words, the gospel, the epistles, and the revelation of John were written last.

The Gospel of John: Believe

The gospels of Matthew, Mark, and Luke, which precede that of John, present various aspects of the Lord Jesus. But it is John in his gospel who shows us the highest and most spiritual aspect about the Son of God coming to this earth. John seems to set everyone aside, both the Jews and the people of the world, in order to focus our attention on the knowledge of the Lord Jesus Himself through whom we may have eternal life. Indeed, the gospel of John

153

is full of "believe"—he who believes has eternal life. This is its theme and also its emphasis. The purpose of his gospel is to convince us that men not only should repent, be baptized, take up the cross and follow the Lord, but also should believe in the Lord so as to receive eternal life. It is in this gospel that we find a most precious word of our Lord: "Verily, verily, I say unto you, He that heareth my word, and believeth him that sent me, hath eternal life, and cometh not into judgment, but hath passed out of death into life" (John 5:24). Who is it that has passed out of death into life? It is he who hears and believes. Whoever hears and believes has passed from death into life.

Of the four gospels, the door of the gospel is opened the widest in John. He shows us how men, by believing, may have eternal life. These are born, not of blood, nor of the will of the flesh, nor of the will of man, but of God (John 1:13). Who are these people? They are those who have received the Lord Jesus. All who have believed in the name of the Lord are born of God. John opens to us a definite and wide door: he who believes has eternal life and does not come into judgment but has passed out of death into life.

The Epistle of John: Love

It is marvelous that the epistles written by Paul, Peter, and other apostles interpret the gospel of God so ably. They show us clearly that those who receive obtain grace. The epistles are clearer, more direct, and more obvious than the gospels. John's epistles too, the last written, show us a definite and clear way. But John's writings differ from others. The gospels other than John's stress our practical life or conduct before God, but his gospel emphasizes faith before God. The epistles other than John's focus on faith before God, but his epistle dwells on our practical life or conduct before God. The gospel of John shows us how to receive eternal life by faith; it surpasses the other gospels in the presentation of the glad tidings in both straightforwardness and clarity. When all the epistles speak of faith, the epistle of John deals with love. When other epistles affirm how those who believe will be justified, forgiven, and cleansed, John's asserts that the believing ones must show evidence of their faith.

When we preach the gospel, we tell people that he who believes has eternal life, for he has passed out of death into life. But we should also challenge those who do believe as to whether they have the witness in them that they have passed from death into life.

If you question people, asking how they know they have eternal life, many will tell you it is because the Word of God says so. Such an answer is too vague. John in his epistle shows us that if anyone says he has life, he must give evidence of it. If he affirms that he belongs to God, his affirmation needs to be backed up by a clear testimony.

People may speak according to their mental knowledge, saying, "I believe; therefore I have eternal life." They reduce, "Believes, has eternal life," into a formula. If they are asked how they know they have eternal life, they will answer, "Is it not stated in the third chapter of the gospel of John?" This is not good enough, for their words betray a lack of personal conviction. After they have heard the gospel of God's grace, they attempt to make their salvation sure by using a formula. They postulate as follows: (1) I have heard the gospel, (2) I understand, (3) I believe, and

(4) I know I have eternal life. How do they know? Because the Bible says so. This kind of salvation is too technical. It is therefore undependable.

How, then, are we to judge whether a man's faith is true or false? How do we know if it is living or procedural? Remember, the apostle John had this very same problem. Yes, the gospel of grace must be preached. And the way of salvation is extremely simple: believe and be saved; contact God and have eternal life. This we must proclaim. However, it is inevitable that there will be pretenders; there will be a mixed multitude.

As there were fake brethren during Paul's lifetime, so there were during John's, and so there are today. Some call themselves brethren, but actually they are not. They profess to belong to God, yet they have no life. They slip into the church by way of doctrine, of knowledge, or of formula. By what means are we to discern whether or not they truly are the Lord's? The epistle of John helps us solve this problem. John shows us what is the evidence of a true brother. He shows what kind of people have life and what kind have not.

1. THE CONSCIOUSNESS OF LOVE

There are only two places in the Bible where the phrase "passed out of death into life" is used. Let us compare these two places:

"Verily, verily, I say unto you. He that heareth my word, and believeth him that sent me, hath eternal life, and cometh not into judgment, but hath passed out of death into life" (John 5:24). He who believes has passed out of death into life.

"We know that we have passed out of death into life, because we love the brethren" (1 John 3:14). Love of the brethren is evidence of having passed out of death into life.

There may be many people with whom you are friends or whom you especially like or respect, but for your brother or your sister, born of the same mother, you reserve an unexplainable sensation, a different consciousness. You feel, "This is my brother, born into my family." This consciousness we call love. Such a consciousness speaks of the fact that someone belongs to the family.

Likewise, here is a person whose action and manner do not please you; his background, family, education, and position are so different from yours. But, in spite of thousands of differences, you feel within you an unspeakable sensation, a wonderful consciousness that he is your brother, even closer than a brother in the flesh. Why? Because he has believed in the Lord Jesus. Such consciousness within you serves as evidence to you that you have passed out of death into life.

It may be quite difficult to distinguish on the basis of faith whether a person has truly believed in the Lord or is merely pretending to believe; whether he believes with his heart or just with his mind; whether he has really met the Lord or has only gone through a formula. But to discern on the basis of love is quite easy. Even John, who wrote so much about faith, found it hard to differentiate between true and false faith. He therefore used love to divide the true and the false. Whoever has the consciousness of love is a child of God; whoever lacks this consciousness is not a child of God. Every child of God will naturally have an unspeakable sensation toward another believer—as if he is closer than a brother. He who possesses this consciousness is a true believer.

Something in you witnesses to the truthfulness of your faith. Out of the faith that you have issues an unspeakable love. This brotherly love is quite unique, for it has no cause other than the fact that someone is a brother. You do not love him because he agrees with you. It is natural for people who have the same interest or the same outlook to love one another. But the one you love is different from you in education, temperament, background, and viewpoint. You love him simply because he is a believer even as you are. You are brethren; therefore you have fellowship. There is an indescribable feeling, an unexplainable sensation toward each other. This consciousness is the evidence of your having passed out of death into life. If I love the brethren, I know I have passed out of death into life.

2. THE LIFE OF LOVE

By faith you meet God, pass out of death into life, and become a member of God's house. You are born again and have become a part of God's family. Faith draws you to the brethren as well as to the Father. It gives you the knowledge of God that you may believe in Him and receive life from Him. Soon after you receive life, you discover that there are many others who have also received this life. Instinctively, this life within you pulls you to those who possess the same life as you. You like to be near them, and you delight in having fellowship with them. You love them spontaneously.

I wish you to take special note of this: the life which we get is not just the life of the only begotten Son of God. If that were the life He gave us, we might not have the love of the brethren. But what we receive is also the life of the firstborn Son of God; this life is the portion of all sons of God. Therefore, it is but natural for us to love the brethren. This love toward the brethren proves that we indeed have life. Hence, faith leads us to God; God gives us life; life inspires us to love the brethren; and the love of the brethren proves to us that we have passed out of death into life.

John's gospel tells us that by believing we may pass out of death into life; his epistle shows us that those who have passed out of death into life love the brethren. God has so ordained that by faith we come out of death into life, and that by passing out of death into life we love. By our loving the brethren, we ourselves are assured that we have indeed passed out of death into life. This, therefore, becomes the acid test for God's children. The brethren must love one another; only if we love one another are we truly brethren. If we do not love one another, we are not brethren. If we do not love the brethren, we are not begotten of God. One may confess with his mouth that he believes, but before God his faith is not real since he does not have love toward the brethren.

We must see this before God: the love of the brethren is the evidence of faith. May I repeat that there is no other way to discern the truth or falsity of a person's faith. The more perfect the presentation of the gospel is, the greater the danger of counterfeit. The more thorough the preaching of the gospel is, the easier for people to simulate it. The fuller the gospel is of grace, the greater the number of half-hearted participants. Consequently, we need to find a way to distinguish false faith from true faith. As indicated in the Bible, the way to do this lies not in examining faith, but by observing love. As John shows, this will judge faith. If faith is real, there will be love. The absence of love means the lack of faith. Where love is, there must be faith. So do not ascertain faith by looking into faith. View faith through love; then all will be clear.

It is not the workers alone who wonder if a person's faith

is real or false. Many new believers themselves ask how they can be sure if their faith is real. If it is faulty, they cannot be sure of having eternal life. So they want to know their actual condition before God. The answer to this question lies in whether or not there is love.

If you have truly believed in God and have life in you, you will naturally be attracted to the brethren. Your love for Christians will be spontaneous; you will feel they are closer to you than your brethren in the flesh, more intimate than the best of your friends. This brotherly affinity is ingrained. You find an inscrutable sensation surge within you which makes you love your brother and love to be with him. Thus do you know you have passed out of death into life. You have the witness within you as well as in the Word of God.

You who have brothers and sisters according to the flesh—how do you know these are your brothers and sisters? Have you asked a physician to examine your blood? How, then, are you assured of their being your brothers and sisters? Let me tell you one thing: you do not need any outside proof because the witness of an inward attraction is sufficient. Within you, there is an instinct which mysteriously tells you which are your brothers and your sisters.

True Christians are begotten of God. To ascertain whether or not a person is a Christian, only a simple question need be asked: do you have a special consciousness, a strange attraction toward the other children of God?

The life which God has given you is not an independent life. It pulls you toward those with the same life. It constrains you to love and to sense a closeness with them. If you possess such a feeling, you know that you have passed out of death into life. It is exceedingly important that you do have such an unusual feeling toward the children of God.

3. THE THOUGHT OF LOVE

"He that saith he is in the light and hateth his brother, is in the darkness even until now. He that loveth his brother abideth in the light, and there is no occasion of stumbling in him. But he that hateth his brother is in the darkness, and walketh in the darkness, and knoweth not whither he goeth, because the darkness hath blinded his eyes" (1 John 2:9-11). Is it not very clear that whether or not one is a brother, whether he is in the light or in the darkness, can be determined by how he treats his brother?

If there is a brother here—and you know he is a brother—yet you hate him in your heart, this sufficiently proves that you are not a Christian. Suppose there are five brothers here. Of these, you confess that you love four but hate one. Let me tell you, you are not a brother. The love of the brethren does not mean loving the loveable or loving those whom you prefer. It means loving a person simply because he is a brother. That is the sole reason for loving him.

The passage just given states that he who hates his brother abides in darkness and walks in darkness. In other words, the Bible refutes the possibility of ever hating a brother. Should you know he is a brother and yet hate him, you will be compelled to acknowledge, "Lord, I am not Yours! O God, I am not Your child, for I live in darkness!"

"In this the children of God are manifest, and the children of the devil: whosoever doeth not righteousness is not of God, neither he that loveth not his brother" (1 John

3:10). People on earth are divided into two groups: the children of God and the children of the devil. Likewise, there are only two fathers: God is a Father, and the devil is a father. It is extremely easy to distinguish God from the devil. But the problem may be in differentiating between the children of God and the children of the devil. According to the word given here, this should not present too much of a problem. The distinction may be made on two counts: (1) "whosoever doeth not righteousness is not of God"—he who does not practice righteousness in his outward conduct is not of God; (2) "neither he that loveth not his brother"—he who does not love his brother is proven to not be a brother and, therefore, not a child of God. On the contrary, he is a child of the devil because he does not possess that inward consciousness of love.

To judge the reality of a brother, one needs only to see whether he has the consciousness of love within him. This is what the world calls nature. In our nature, in our bones and marrow, there is a natural affinity. Whoever is born of God finds this natural attraction most distinct and most strong. It is therefore evident that a man who professes to be a child of God and yet hates his brother cannot be of God.

4. The Charge of Love

"For this is the message which ye heard from the beginning, that we should love one another . . . We know that we have passed out of death into life, because we love the brethren. He that loveth not abideth in death" (1 John 3:11, 14).

The love we are talking about is not ordinary love but the love of the brethren. He who lacks this love, as the Bible indicates, yet abides in death. If I am cold to a person, void of any feeling toward him, I know he is a stranger who has no relationship to me. But if I sense an affinity within me, I know he is my brother. Before I trusted in the Lord, I did not have the slightest feeling or attraction toward believers. Today if I still have no inward sense of affinity toward them, I am afraid my faith is faulty, for he who loves not abides in death. I was dead, and now I am still in death. Faith, therefore, is evidenced by love. The reality of faith is judged by the proof of love. Whoever believes in God has love for the brethren. If love is not evident, that person is proven to be yet in death and thus no different from unbelievers.

"Whosoever hateth his brother is a murderer: and ye know that no murderer hath eternal life abiding in him" (1 John 3:15). It is absolutely unbelievable that one who believes in the Lord would murder. He who hates his brother is a murderer, and a murderer does not have eternal life in him. Consequently, no one who has eternal life would hate his brother. By not hating his brother, one proves himself to have love in him.

Let us now consider what is meant by hating one's brother. There are certain things that may be permissible to God's children, but hatred is not one of them. If a brother displays an unpleasant temperament, I may dislike him in my heart. If he commits a sin deserving excommunication, I may perhaps deal angrily with his case. I may severely reprimand a brother who has done something nasty. But how can I be a saved person if I hate another brother? Just to hate *one* person is proof enough that one is not of God.

The life within all children of God is so rich that they can love every brother and every sister. Such love is spontaneous in all who belong to God. There is no difference between loving one brother and loving all the brethren. The same love is shown to the one as to the other. He is loved because he is a brother. The number of persons has no bearing here. Brotherly love is love of all the brethren. If a person hates one brother sufficiently, it shows that brotherly love is not in him.

This is a most serious problem today. If a brother can offend another brother, defraud him, even hate him, we can do nothing but say; "O God, have mercy! Here is one who is not saved." This is most serious, is it not?

Whenever you want to find out whether a new believer is really saved, you only need to ask him if he loves the brethren. He who hates his brother is a murderer. If a person murders just one person, not all the people in the world, he is a murderer. If he hates his brother, he becomes a murderer, and a murderer does not have eternal life abiding in him.

Suppose there is a brother sitting near me here. I know he is a brother; yet my feelings toward him are not at all positive. Within me, I only desire to attack him and see him fall. This single incident proves beyond doubt that I am one who has never met life. I do not need to harbor such an evil desire toward many brothers in order to attest to the absence of life in me. The very fact that I can conceive such a pure hatred toward only one brother verifies that I am not of the Lord.

Suppose I have a controversy with a brother, but I do not hate him. There are many things that he does which I strongly oppose, but I do not hate him. I may have to do things which will hurt his feelings, yet I can still tell him, "Brother, I do not like to hurt you; but, in order to be obedient to God, I have to do these things. I know it will hurt you, but I have no alternative." I can get angry with what he has done, but I cannot hate him. I may strongly reprimand him, but still there is love in me, no hate. Should it be that I have to go to the church about this brother, as described in Matthew 18, my motive is to gain him, to restore him. If my desire were his destruction, if I were void of the desire for restoration, I could not be reckoned as a brother. In Matthew 18 the brother tells the church because he wishes to gain his brother. The question is: is my desire purely destructive or is it restorative? If I tell the church in order to destroy, I betray myself as having never been saved. Once I have life, I can never destroy any brother. How can I murder my brother? This is indeed a serious matter.

What is brotherly love? How does Paul explain it? In 1 Corinthians 5, there was a wicked man whom Paul urged the church to drive away. Since they did not take any action, the apostle in the Spirit delivers that man in the name of the Lord Jesus to Satan for the destruction of the flesh. How very serious it is for Paul, before God, to deliver a brother to Satan for the destruction of the flesh. Why does he act this way? "That his spirit may be saved in the day of the Lord Jesus." This temporary destruction of the flesh is for the sake of saving him from eternal loss. The result of this drastic course of action is seen in 2 Corinthians. Here, the person excommunicated in 1 Corinthians 5 has produced a repentance that needs not to be repented of. Let us therefore remember that telling the church, as in Matthew 18, is for the sake of restoration, and that excommunication, as seen in 1 Corinthians 5, is for the same purpose.

The judgment of Joshua on Achan is also full of love. "And Joshua said unto Achan, My son, give, I pray thee, glory to Jehovah, the God of Israel . . ." (Josh. 7:19).

165

When he spoke to Achan, his spirit was full of brotherly love. If one's heart intention is to get rid of a brother because the latter is so wicked, he knows nothing of brotherly love.

The time David wept was when Absalom died. Although Absalom was rebellious, he still was a son. David mourned the death of Saul, but he cried at the death of Absalom. Saul had been his king, but Absalom was his rebellious son. The battle must be fought, rebellion must be punished, yet cry David must. Though judgment was necessary, tears could not be withheld.

Brothers and sisters, if there is judgment without tears, then there is manifestly no knowledge of brotherly love. If there is condemnation but no distress, then there is no understanding of brotherhood. If there is nothing but reproach and destruction, it is evident that there is no love. Should hate alone be present, he who hates is a murderer and does not have eternal life abiding in him.

J. N. Darby has spoken well about this. When he was asked about the matter of excommunication, his first word was, "I think it is the most horrible thing in the whole world for a forgiven sinner to excommunicate another forgiven sinner." Indeed, there can be nothing more wicked and horrible than this. Do you see an attitude here? You touch something out of life in this. Things may be done, but there may not be hatred. To hate a brother is to murder him, regardless of whether that hate is with or without a cause.

To know whether or not a person is a brother, you must examine to see if he has life; and to examine life, you look to see if he has pure hate toward another brother. If he has, he is definitely not of God and has never known life.

Let us be careful lest we do things against love. Do not

offend a brother. Rather, love one another. Do not allow brotherly love to leave you because of wounds received, for this will have serious consequences. God has put love of the brethren in us that we may help and serve one another. This love should grow stronger in us as the days go on.

"Hereby know we love, because he laid down his life for us: and we ought to lay down our lives for the brethren" (1 John 3:16). It is not easy to know what love is, but in the Lord's laying down His life for us, we can see love. Love caused our Lord to give His life for us. Thus do we know love.

"We ought to lay down our lives for the brethren." To love the brethren is to sacrifice oneself for all the brothers and sisters in order to serve and to perfect them. When it is needed, we are ready to lay down our lives for them.

"But whoso hath the world's goods, and beholdeth his brother in need, and shutteth up his compassion from him, how doth the love of God abide in him?" (1 John 3:17). As to him who has earthly means and yet shuts up his compassion toward his brother in need, John says, "How doth the love of God abide in him?" He does not say how can the love of the brethren abide in him, but, how does the love of God abide in him. Why? The love of God is the love of the brethren, and the love of the brethren is the love of God. Do not deceive yourself by saying, "Though I do not love the brothers and sisters, yet I love God; I do not love my brothers and sisters, but I do love my parents." From where does our relationship with our brothers and sisters come? It comes from our parents. If we are not related to our brothers and sisters, we are not related to our parents either. By forsaking the brethren, we throw away love to the parents.

167

"My little children, let us not love in word, neither with the tongue; but in deed and truth. . . . And this is his commandment, that we should believe in the name of his Son Jesus Christ, and love one another, even as he gave us commandment" (1 John 3:18, 23). This is the charge of God: we have believed, now we must love. God both gives us the command to love as well as the love itself. He first bestows love on us, and then He charges us to love one another. Today we should apply this love which God has given us by loving one another in accordance with His commandment. Since He has put love in us, let us pay special attention today to use it according to its nature and not to hurt or destroy it.

5. THE REALITY OF LOVE

"Beloved, let us love one another: for love is of God; and every one that loveth is begotten of God, and knoweth God. He that loveth not knoweth not God; for God is love" (1 John 4:7–8).

Why should we love one another? Because love is of God. Whoever loves is begotten of God, and whoever does not love, does not know God. God is love, and love comes from God. When He begat us, He implanted love in us. We did not have this love in the past, but now we possess it. It is from God. And it is given to all who are begotten of God that we may love one another.

Whoever is begotten of God has life. John tells us that this life is God Himself and God is love. For this reason, he who is begotten of God has this love born in him. The gospel of John emphasizes faith, and the life of faith is a life which does not sin. But we must understand that "does not sin" is negative. The Bible never says that God does not sin, for this sounds too negative. Here in the epistle of

John, the Bible stresses love; that is, the life we have received from God is the life of love. Love is positive, for God is love.

Whoever is begotten of God has this love in him. It is first manifest among brothers and sisters. We can love one another because we are all born of God and we each have this love in us. It would be surprising if we did not love one another. We bow our heads reverently, saying that God's children are able to love one another. The life we now have is new and powerful, for, before God asks us to love, He first gives us love. Being born of God, we should learn to love the brethren. In the time of need, we should be ready to lay down everything for our brethren.

"Beloved, if God so loved us, we also ought to love one another. No man hath beheld God at any time: if we love one another, God abideth in us, and his love is perfected in us" (1 John 4:11-12). These verses show us the relationship between loving one another and loving God. If we love one another, God's love is perfected in us. In other words, though we do love God, we seem to lack the opportunity to show that love, so God has put many brothers and sisters in our way now to be the practical targets of our love. These brethren give us the opportunity to realize our love toward God. Do not brag of your love of God, but learn to love the brethren. Bragging of love is empty, but the love of God is manifest in love of the brethren.

"And we know and have believed the love which God hath in us. God is love; and he that abideth in love abideth in God, and God abideth in him" (1 John 4:16). This is the second time in this chapter that "God is love" has been mentioned. Since God is love, He expects us to love the brethren and to abide in love. We have no need to say that we abide in God, for if we abide in love we abide in God.

"Herein is love made perfect with us, that we may have boldness in the day of judgment; because as he is, even so are we in this world. There is no fear in love: but perfect love casteth out fear, because fear hath punishment; and he that feareth is not made perfect in love" (1 John 4:17–18). I do not know if you see the preciousness of these words. This is the only place in the Bible where it tells us how we may have boldness before the judgment seat of Christ. The secret John passes on to us is to abide in love. Whoever abides in love abides in God. Love is thus made perfect in us, and we may have boldness in the day of judgment.

Therefore, let us have no other mind toward brothers and sisters than that of love. We are minded to love them, to win them, and to seek their highest good. Let there be no jealousy or hatred, but only love. Such exercise on our part is profitable, until one day our whole being will abide in love and love will abide in us. Then we may be able to cast out all fear even while we live on earth. If we love, we fear not; with love in us, we have boldness before the judgment seat of Christ. This life will so operate among the brethren that fear will be totally cast out. The fruit of the Holy Spirit—love—will be preserved till the day of judgment. We may stand before the judgment seat without fear, for as He is, so are we in the world. How wonderful it is to be without fear, without the fear of death or the fear of God.

We have already seen that to love the brethren is to love God. By loving the brethren, our love of God is made perfect. We may love our brethren to such a perfect state that we nurse no fear of the brethren in our heart. Our entire inward being is transformed, for the sense of fear is gone. Do you see the parallelism? Loving God is loving the brethren. To not fear the brethren is to not fear God. In order to love God, we must love the brethren on earth. Because we love the brethren today and harbor no fear toward them, we shall one day stand before the judgment seat of Christ without fear of God. Those who love the brethren shall alone have boldness in the day of judgment, for they have no fear. This is most marvelous indeed.

"If a man say, I love God, and hateth his brother, he is a liar: for he that loveth not his brother whom he hath seen, cannot love God whom he hath not seen. And this commandment have we from him, that he who loveth God love his brother also" (1 John 4:20–21). John shows us that in loving the brethren, we love God. If we cannot love the brethren whom we see, how can we love God whom we cannot see? If we love God, we will love the brethren. This is the commandment we have from God.

The life which God has given us is a life of love. We should not focus our attention on the "sin not" aspect of the life of God and forget to remember the "love" aspect of the same life. In the past we have emphasized the "sin not" aspect of God's life; now we will equally stress the "love" aspect. God has first loved us and He has put the love in us by which we love the brethren. Hereafter we must learn not to offend love. There may be many times when you will have to say to your brother, "Brother, though I may hurt you in this matter, I have no pleasure in it. I do it with reason; it is for God's sake, and also for your sake."

Suppose, after you have believed in the Lord, you one day feel constrained to go out and preach the gospel. Your parents will not give their permission, so you quarrel with them. To preach the gospel is good, but you have offended love. You should see that you must obey the Lord on the one hand and speak humbly to your parents on the other hand, saying, "I truly am willing to obey you. I would that I could listen to you and not preach the gospel, but I cannot because God has commanded me to go." Thus can you preach the gospel without sinning against love. Many brothers and sisters love the right things yet have risked offending love. Their attitude is too hard; they have grown excessive in righteousness but deficient in love. So, we must learn to obey God without sinning against love under any circumstance.

We should learn from the very beginning how to be righteous, but we should never lose love. Do you see the necessity of this balance? A new believer should do what ought to be done, but he must be careful not to offend love. Even when he disagrees with people, his attitude must be gentle and full of love. He should be able to say, "Brother, I wish I could see it as you do, but I must obey what God has shown me." Do not strive with others. Never compromise God's Word, but also never offend love. On the one hand obey, and on the other hand love. I believe there are many among us who do walk in this straight path. What a failure it is to the testimony of God's children if their obedience is mixed with noisy striving and unseemly feelings!

6. THE ABSOLUTENESS OF LOVE

"Whosoever believeth that Jesus is the Christ is begotten of God: and whosoever loveth him that begat loveth him also that is begotten of him" (1 John 5:1). How very precious this word is. It is so natural to love those who are begotten of God if you love Him who begets you. There is absolutely no possibility that you can love God without having the slightest consciousness of love toward your brethren.

"Hereby we know that we love the children of God, when we love God and do his commandments" (1 John 5:2). It is clear that if we love God we will keep His commandments. But if we try to love men as well as God, we may find we are unable to keep God's commandments. It is true that whoever loves God keeps His commandments, but we cannot say that he who loves the children of God necessarily keeps God's commandments.

For example, suppose you are constrained to do a certain thing for God. Many of God's children will say to you, "If you love us, you will not do it, for you will hurt us if you do." To love God, you must do it; but to love the brethren, you may not do it. How very strange, then, is John's word, "Hereby we know that we love the children of God, when we love God and do His commandments." This says that if you do not keep God's commandments you cannot say you love the children of God. If God constrains you to do a certain thing, you must do it, not only for the love of God but also for the love of the brethren. If you do not obey, those of God's children who tried to hinder you will not choose to obey either. In hindering you from obedience, they actually deprive themselves of the opportunity to obey God.

When you keep all the commandments of God, you show evidence of loving the brethren. By walking in this way of obedience, you open it to all the children of God that they too may walk in it. Should you refrain from walking in it for fear of hurting them, you close the way of obedience to them. Therefore, learn to love God and keep all His commandments; by this, your love toward the brethren is manifested. Does any child of God, for the sake of loving his parents, disbelieve the Lord because they have forbidden him to believe? If so, he is not acting in love; for although his parents may be angry with him if he believes, he nonetheless has opened a way for them to believe also.

More people are won by love than by hate. In your contact with people, do not offend them. True, it is necessary for you to obey God and to hearken to His commandments, but do not offend people by your attitude or your word. Convince them that you do not purposely offend them; it is only because you are constrained by God that you do so. Your attitude must not be sour or hard; it should be full of meekness and gentleness. In this way, we believe many will be attracted to the Lord. Remember, love gains more people than hate. Hate drives off people, but love draws them. Therefore, do not hate.

PRIESTHOOD

There is an office mentioned in the Bible called the priesthood. The priesthood is a group of people wholly separated from the world in order to serve God. They have no profession or duty other than the task of serving God. They are priests.

The History of the Priests

From the book of Genesis on, God has had His priests. Melchizedek was God's first priest. During the time of Abraham, Melchizedek had already separated himself for the service of God. From Melchizedek till after the nation of Israel was established, there were always priests.

When the Lord Jesus was on earth and even after His departure, the priesthood continued. And after His ascension, the Bible shows us that the Lord Jesus became a priest before God. In other words, He is in heaven ministering fully unto God.

The priesthood continues on throughout the dispensation of the church. After that, those who have part in the first resurrection will be priests of God and of Christ and

shall reign with Him for a thousand years (Rev. 20:6).
Thus, in the millennial kingdom, God's children will
continue being priests of God and of Christ. They will be
kings to the world and priests to God. The nature of the
priesthood will remain unchanged, for the priests will still
serve God.

Even when the new heavens and the new earth come,
the priesthood will not fade away. In New Jerusalem all
God's children and all God's servants will do nothing but
serve Him.

Here is a most wonderful thing: the priesthood commenced with Melchizedek—who is without father, without
mother, without genealogy, having neither beginning of
days nor end of life—and it continues on through the
millennium. Its service extends to the eternity to come.

The Kingdom of Priests

Although at first only Melchizedek was priest, the
purpose of God is for all His people to be priests—not just
a few of them.

After the Israelites came out of Egypt and to Mount
Sinai, God spoke to them through Moses, saying, "Ye shall
be unto me a kingdom of priests, and a holy nation" (Ex.
19:6). Why does it say a *kingdom* of priests? For one reason
only: that the whole nation should be priests. Not one
person in the country was to be just an ordinary person; all
were priests. This is God's purpose.

When God chose Israel to be His people, He set this one
purpose before them: their nation was to be different from
all the other nations because theirs was to be a kingdom of
priests. All the people in the kingdom were to be priests.
Every person's occupation was to serve God. God delights

to choose people to serve Him; He likes to have them occupied with His business on earth.

At Mount Sinai God informed the people of Israel that He would set them up as a kingdom of priests. This is truly a beautiful thing. We call Great Britain a naval country, the United States of America a gold country, China a nation of etiquette, and India a philosophical nation, but here we find a nation which is called a kingdom of priests. In this nation everyone is a priest, the men as well as the women, the adults as well as the children. They do nothing but serve God. This becomes their sole profession. Is it not wonderful?

After God told them that He would establish them as a kingdom of priests, He called Moses to ascend the mountain in order to receive the Ten Commandments written on two tables. Moses remained on the mountain forty days. With His own hand God wrote the commandments: "Thou shalt have no other gods before me"; "Thou shalt not make unto thee a graven image"; and so forth.

But when the people saw that Moses delayed to come down from the mount, they gathered themselves to Aaron and said to him, "Up, make us gods, which shall go before us; for as for this Moses . . . we know not what is become of him" (Ex. 32:1). Aaron listened to them and made them a golden calf. And they said, "These are thy gods, O Israel, which brought thee up out of the land of Egypt" (Ex. 32:4).

They began to worship the idol and sat down to eat and drink, and rose up to play. They rejoiced greatly because they could see the god which they had made of molten gold. The God whom Moses had led them to know had certain disadvantages for He was invisible and not easily found. And now, even the Moses who taught them to

177

worship God was not to be found. So it was very convenient for them to worship the golden calf, for it could be seen. In other words, though God had intended to make them His priests, before that was ever realized, they had already turned themselves into priests of the golden calf. God purposed to make them a kingdom of priests, but before they were initiated, they had turned aside to worship an idol. They had another god and another worship.

Man's natural concept of God is always such that he inclines to make his own god. He likes to worship the god of his own hand instead of accepting the authority and position of God the Creator.

The Priestly Tribe

God told Moses to go down from the mount, so Moses turned and went down with the two tables of testimony, the Ten Commandments, in his hands. As he drew near the camp and saw the condition of the people, his wrath waxed hot, and he broke those two tables beneath the mount. Then he stood in the gate of the camp and said, "Whoso is on Jehovah's side, let him come unto me." And all the sons of Levi gathered themselves together to him. And he said to them, "Thus saith Jehovah the God of Israel. Put ye every man his sword upon his thigh, and go to and fro from gate to gate throughout the camp, and slay every man his brother, and every man his companion, and every man his neighbor" (Ex. 32:26–27). They were to kill everyone they met who had worshiped the golden calf. They must totally disregard any personal relationship; they must slay indiscriminately.

Many felt this charge was too harsh. Who had the heart

to slay his own brother, his own friends? Eleven of the twelve tribes remained inactive. The cost was too high for them. Only the tribe of Levi drew their swords, went to and fro from gate to gate throughout the camp, and slew about three thousand men on that day. Those slain were their own brothers, relatives, and friends.

Let us take special note here: After this incident of the golden calf, God immediately informed Moses that hereafter the nation of Israel could not be a kingdom of priests. Though this was not explicitly stated, yet it was implicitly understood, for henceforth God gave the privilege of being priests to the tribe of Levi alone. That which was originally intended for the whole nation of Israel was now given to the house of Aaron of the tribe of Levi.

From that time on, there existed two classes of people of God: one class was the people of God and the other class was the priests of God. God's original design was to make every one of His people a priest. He did not intend to divide them into people and priests. The whole kingdom would be priests. God's people and God's priests would be one and the same. Who were God's people? Who were God's priests? Whoever was one of God's people was also God's priest and whoever was God's priest was one of God's people. But, due to the fact that so many loved the world and succumbed to human affection and forsook faithfulness to the Lord and worshiped idols, God was forced to take the measure of dividing His priests from His people. If any person does not love the Lord more than father, mother, wife, children, brother, sister, and all, he is unfit to be a disciple of the Lord. Alas, too many do not pay the price and fulfill the conditions.

At first there was a kingdom of priests, but now there was a tribe of priests. What was originally intended to be for a nation was now realized in a family. The priesthood was confined to a family instead of a nation. In the tribe of Levi, God's people and God's priests were one—that is, God's people were God's priests. But the other eleven tribes, though they were God's people, could not be God's priests. This was indeed a most serious matter. And is it not still a matter of deep seriousness if a person believes on the Lord and yet fails to function as a priest?

The Priesthood

From the time of the book of Exodus till the coming of the Lord Jesus to the earth, no one could do the work of a priest other than those who were of the tribe of Levi. No one else could offer sacrifices to God, for God would not accept them. The sacrifices had to be made through the priests. Likewise, no one could approach God to confess sin; he must confess through the priest. He could not even separate himself from the world, for he had no authority to touch the anointing oil; the priest alone could anoint and set him apart. No ordinary person was allowed to do any spiritual service; the priest performed everything in his stead.

In the Old Testament there was a special feature concerning the Israelites: God was distant from them; not everyone could contact Him. Instead, there was a priesthood formed as an intermediary class. Man could not go to God directly. If the people of Israel wanted to draw near to God, they had to go through the priests. They had no right to commune with God directly. God came to men through the priests, and men went to God through the priests. Between God and man was a mediatorial class, no direct communication.

According to God's original design, this was not necessary. In His original purpose, He was to have direct communication with man and man with Him. But now the situation was changed. Now it was not just God and the people; it was God, the priests, and the people. The people went to God via the priests and God came to the people through the priests. The contact had become indirect.

The Priesthood Changed

For about fifteen hundred years, from Moses till Christ, the people of God were not able to present themselves directly to God. Only one family was chosen to be priests. In order to approach God, every person must pass through them. If anyone dared to draw near to God by himself, he would be smitten to death. During that period, the function of the priest was of tremendous importance. How noble the priesthood was! How great! But then, suddenly, the New Covenant came and under it men could be saved and redeemed directly. Suddenly we hear the word, "Ye also, as living stones, are built up a spiritual house, to be a holy priesthood, to offer up spiritual sacrifices, acceptable to God through Jesus Christ" (1 Pet. 2:5).

Peter tells us that Christ is the foundation of the church. He is the stone rejected by the builders that has become the head of the corner. Through Him, we too have become living stones to be joined and built together to be both a spiritual temple and God's holy priesthood. The voice from heaven informs us that all saved ones are God's priests. All who have become living stones and are related to the spiritual temple are the priests of God.

All of a sudden, the promise which had been laid aside

for fifteen hundred years was again taken up by God. What the Israelites lost, the church gained. Universal priesthood was lost to Israel, but today, with the New Covenant, the voice from heaven comes to tell us that all saved ones are priests.

"And he made us to be a kingdom, to be priests unto his God and Father" (Rev. 1:6). Originally, the whole nation of Israel were priests but they soon disqualified themselves. The church, however, is today a kingdom of priests. What the Israelites lost after worshiping the golden calf is now fully gained by the church through the Lord Jesus. All who are in the church are priests. God's destined kingdom of priests is thus wholly realized.

What is meant by the church being a kingdom of priests or by all in the church being priests? This simply implies that the occupation of all who have received God's grace is one: to serve God. As I have said before to the young people, the occupation of a medical doctor who has believed in the Lord is not medicine, of a nurse is not nursing, of a teacher is not teaching, of a farmer is not farming, of a businessman is not business. Remember, when you became a Christian, your profession underwent a complete change. All Christians have only one profession and that is, to serve God. From now on, I am God's priest. Outwardly I may be busily occupied in various things, but inwardly I am before God, serving Him. Everything is done with this as the spiritual objective.

All Christians, then, are engaged in one occupation— serving God. He who is a physician should not aspire to fame; rather, his practice as a doctor should serve only to sustain his physical life. His real profession now is that he is a priest before God. The same applies to a professor. He should not seek for renown, to be an outstanding professor;

he should seek to be a good priest of God. His teaching becomes an avocation; his main vocation is to serve God. So this same service should govern Christians of all professions—laborers, farmers, whatever. Their one and only profession, in fact, is to serve God.

From the day you become a Christian, you should lay aside your ambitions and plans. You should not seek to be an outstanding person in your particular field. As a Christian, you should have only one ambition, that of Paul's—to be well-pleasing to the Lord (2 Cor. 5:9). You should have no other ambition than this. Any worldly future you might once have had is smashed forever. Now you must be prepared to be one who serves the Lord.

The Glory of the Priests

During the early days of my Christian life, I thought it would take quite an effort to lead a young believer to serve God. I thought I had to persuade, plead, and beg. But God's thought is totally different from ours. It was because the Israelites sinned that God took the priesthood away from them. In other words, serving God is the highest glory and greatest privilege He can bestow on man. If a person should fail, God will take this privilege away from him. He has no intention to persuade, to beg, or to seek man's pleasure. It is man's glory, not God's, that he can be a priest to God.

Recall how, in Exodus, when some people offered strange fire, they were burned to death. If an ordinary person entered the holy place or offered sacrifices, he would be stricken to death. No one except the priests could draw near to God. From God's viewpoint, to make men become priests shows His confidence in them, imparts glory, and uplifts them. If any person should attempt according to his own will to be a priest, he would die. Uzzah, who stretched out his fleshly hand to steady the ark when it tilted, was smitten with death.

Sometimes people have the idea that they elevate God by offering their service to Him! Over the past decades, I have many times observed revival meetings where people were begged to serve God. Other times people gave a little money as if they were doing a special favor for God. And sometimes people offered their services to God, but in that same way of doing a favor. For a man to give up a little position in the world seems to imply how much God is being honored by the service of such a one. Let me tell you, this is blindness. This is folly. And this is darkness.

Because God in heaven has called us to be priests, we should crawl on our knees and bow before Him, for we have received such great glory. God has honored us. Is there anything that anyone in this world can offer to God? Yet, it is our greatest glory that God is willing to accept what we offer. For such as we to be privileged to serve God is glory indeed. This truly is grace! This most surely is the gospel! The gospel not only saves us through the Lord Jesus, but also enables us to serve God. How great is this gospel.

The Priesthood Affirmed

Today the church no longer has a restricted priesthood but a universal priesthood. The nation of Israel failed once; the church cannot afford to fail again. Because the Israelites failed, God's people and God's priests were separated; but in the church there must not be such a separation. In the church God's people are God's priests. If there are people, there are priests. There are as many priests as there are brothers and sisters. Every one of us must draw near to God and offer spiritual sacrifices. All should offer the sacrifice of praise, all should take part in spiritual matters. This is not a selective ministry, for all are to serve God. Unless all are involved, it is not the church.

However, today's situation is such that the priesthood is no longer universal. The nation of Israel failed; must the church fail too? During these two thousand years, there have never been as many priests as Christians. In church history, we often see a separation between the priests and the other believers. An intermediary class has come between God and His people. This is the work and the teaching of the Nicolaitans.

I hope brothers and sisters will see this clearly; we cannot allow an intermediary class to exist. We will not accept any group standing between God's children and God, serving as an intermediary priesthood. We ought never to accept that. We know what the church is. In the church every child of God is a priest. We do not ask one or a few to manage spiritual things for us. An intermediary class cannot be accepted in the church.

Take note that our controversy is not with the outward form but with the contents of Christianity. We see today the presence of an intermediary class in Christianity—those who are appointed to serve God while the rest of the people are merely members of the church. Even though the latter are God's children, they yet depend on the former in their approach to God. Not only does such an intermediary class exist, but it is even permitted by many organizations. We, however, cannot accept this intermediary class, for we will not, as the Israelites of old did, forfeit the grace God has given the church under the New Covenant.

Let us, then, get rid of the intermediary class. The best way to abolish it is for everyone to be in that class! We should kneel before the Lord and say, "Lord, I am willing to serve you. I am willing to be a priest."

The idea of an intermediary class comes from the world, from the flesh, from idol worship, and from the love of the world. If, from the beginning, all the brethren would deny the world and its idols, they would be able to offer themselves to God. They would say, "Hereafter I live on earth for the sole purpose of serving God." Quite naturally, then, the intermediary class would dissolve. If every brother and sister realized that serving God is our only occupation, the intermediary class would fade away in no time.

Actually, right from the outset, no mediatorial class should be allowed. It is only through failure and self-will that such a class can ever come into being. It seems to be natural that some serve the Lord and some not. Those who do not may engage in earthly things; those who do take care of spiritual things. The very most the former will do for the latter is to contribute some money. They go about their own businesses as traders, teachers, or physicians and seem to be utterly unconcerned with serving God. Sometimes they may want to be better Christians, so they set aside a certain time in the week to attend church services and to give some money as their offering. In this way the people of God are separated from the priests of God. This ought not to happen. We must realize that as Christians we ought to be fully committed; those who are fully committed are priests.

The Revival of the Priesthood

Let us remember that the peril of Israel has been the peril of the church over these twenty centuries. From the time of the Lord's departure from this world until after the book of Revelation was written, all the children of God were priests. There was no problem in this respect. But, from the end of the first century through the third century, there began to be frequent troubles about it; as yet, though, there was no general problem. Here and there some children of God were unwilling to be priests; generally speaking, however, the universal priesthood of believers was still maintained.

When Rome endorsed Christianity, many people joined in with the believers. At that time there were earthly benefits in professing to be the Lord's since such people would be fellow-believers and brothers to Caesar. The Lord's charge is: "Render therefore unto Caesar the things that are Caesar's; and unto God the things that are God's' (Matt. 22:21). But then people began to say we should give the things of Caesar and the things of God both to God. This seemed to be a big victory for Christianity. But after that, the church began to undergo a big change Formerly, during the Roman persecution, tens of thousands of Christians had suffered martyrdom. It was not easy then to pretend to be a Christian. But now the situation was totally different. It was fashionable to be Christian, for those who believed in the Lord would share the same faith as the emperor. Many, therefore, crowded into Christianity. The number of people greatly increased, but the number of priests did not increase. Why? Because it was possible to join in as a Christian, but it was not possible to join in and serve God.

187

So, in the fourth century, the church went through a drastic change. During this period, many entered the church who were unbelievers, half-believers, or worldly believers. These people had no desire to serve the Lord. Naturally, it was up to some of the spiritual persons to take care of church affairs. So those who were not so deeply concerned told the others, "You better manage the church affairs and serve the Lord, for we are the seculars." The word "secular" was first introduced then, in the fourth century. The result was that one group served God, while many more did not serve Him.

During the first century, at the time of the apostles, every believer served the Lord. But from the fourth century on, many who called themselves God's people also wanted to have the world. They wished to manage their own affairs and keep their positions in society. They were willing to sometimes give a little money, and they thought this would qualify them as Christians. Let the spiritual ones take care of spiritual things was their attitude. Hence the church followed in the footsteps of the nation of Israel in worshiping the golden calf and in having an intermediary class. Not all God's people were priests; indeed, most were just people, not priests.

Even to our present day, Roman Catholic fathers are called priests. The Protestant churches call such people either priests or pastors or ministers. Those who manage earthly affairs are called laymen or people, while those who manage spiritual things are called the clergy or the priests. Once again, the church has priests separate from the people.

I want to show brothers and sisters that, during this last day, it is God's intention to recover things to His original design. He is going the way of recovery. He is going to bring His children to this course. One basic segment of His recovery is for the church to restore the universal priesthood of the believers. All believers are priests as well as people—priests today and priests in the kingdom to come. God wants priests; He wishes all His people to be priests.

The Service of the Priests

To be a Christian is to be a priest. Do not expect anyone to be a priest for you. You yourself are to so function. Since we have no intermediary class among us, no one will substitute himself for you in spiritual things. Let there not be a special class of such workers created in our midst.

If God is gracious to us, we will naturally find all brothers and sisters functioning in the church. All will preach the gospel, all will serve God. The more prevailing the priesthood is, the better the church. If the priesthood is not universal, we have failed God; we have not walked uprightly.

For such as we, who are poor, weak, blind, and crippled, to be accepted by the Lord to be priests is unquestionably our glory. In the Old Testament times, such people could not function as priests. All who were disabled, lame, or with blemishes were barred from service. But today we—the base, the unclean, the dark, and the disabled— are called by God to be priests. Oh, He is Lord! As I have said, I only want to crawl to Him and kneel before Him and tell Him, "Lord, I am happy to serve You, I am glad to be Your servant. That I may come to You is evidence that You have lifted me." Let me tell you, to be a priest is to draw near to God. To be a priest is to have no distance between you and God. To be a priest is to be able to enter directly into His presence. To be a priest means you do not need to wait for help. To be a priest means you can touch God.

If some day the brothers and sisters in every place are found serving God, then in truth will the kingdom of God have come. It will be a kingdom of priests, for all the people will be priests. I look toward this event as a most glorious thing. May we pay whatever price is needed for us to serve God. May we deal with all idols. The Levites paid the price by disregarding their personal affection. Such people are worthy to have the priesthood.

Beloved, in order to know what the priesthood means, we need to understand how God treated the priests in the Old Testament. For God to permit you to draw near to Him and still not die is a tremendous step. The priests alone could eat the showbread; they alone could serve at the altar; they alone could enter the holy place; and they alone could offer sacrifices. Any stranger who tried to enter would die. This clearly indicates that God's acceptance of us is the foundation of the priesthood. Since God has accepted me, I may enter in. Formerly, if anyone dared to enter in, he would die. But today God says, "You may come in!" Do we not want to go in? It would be most surprising if we did not.

We have seen before that it is grace that enables us to serve God—the most abundant grace which God has bestowed upon us. I think that those who really know God will all respond by saying that the grace that has enabled me to serve God is even greater than the grace which has brought me salvation. The dog under the table may eat the crumbs of the bread underneath the table, but it cannot serve the master at the table. To be saved by grace is relatively simple, but to serve by grace is much higher. How foolish one is if he is unaware of that abundant grace which enables him to serve God—as well as to be saved.

Organized Christianity today not only recognizes the presence of an intermediary class but also actually divides God's priests from God's people. If it were merely the failure of one or two persons, it would not constitute a principle. But much of Christianity has accepted the principle of restricted or selective priesthood. She has fallen into the same failure as the Israelites, the separation of people and priests. May we not fall into such a system. May God be gracious to us.

THE BODY OF CHRIST

There are quite a few things we would like to mention in regard to the body of Christ.

Christ, the Church, and the Body

"For no man ever hated his own flesh; but nourisheth and cherisheth it, even as Christ also the church; because we are members of his body" (Eph. 5:29-30. Darby's version adds in brackets, "We are of his flesh and of his bones").

In the Old Testament God shows us how He took a rib out of Adam and built Eve. Eve came out of Adam. Or, to use another expression, Eve was Adam. Similarly, if we ask, "What is the church?" the reply is that the church comes out of Christ. As God built Eve with that which He took out of Adam, so He builds the church with that which is taken out of Christ. Christ has given us not only His power, grace, nature, and will, but also His own body. He has given us His bones and His flesh. He has given Himself to us, just as Adam gave his bone to Eve.

The Bible tells us that Christ is the head of the church, and the church is the body of Christ. Individually, every

Christian is a member of the body of Christ, for every one comes out of Him.

One thing to especially notice is that the body of Christ is on earth. It is on earth, though it does not belong to the earth. It is heavenly, yet it is on earth. Do not think that the body of Christ is in heaven. When Paul persecuted the church, the Lord Jesus challenged him on the road to Damascus, saying, "Saul, Saul, why persecutest thou me?" The word of the Lord here is really wonderful. He did not say, "Saul, Saul, why persecutest thou my disciples?" but He said, "Saul, Saul, why persecutest thou me?" He did not ask, "Saul, Saul, why persecutest thou my people?" or "Why persecutest thou my church?" He simply said, "Saul, Saul, why persecutest thou me?" Thus it was revealed to Paul that the church and Christ are one. The oneness of the church and Christ is of such a nature that to persecute the church is to persecute Christ. Moreover, the incident on the Damascus road indicates that the body of Christ is something on earth. If it were in heaven, it would not be persecuted nor could it be persecuted. But today the church on earth is the body of Christ. Thus Saul could persecute the church.

Many maintain that the manifestation of the body is a heavenly affair, so this manifestation has to wait till we all get to heaven. If this were the case, then Saul could not have persecuted the Lord. But the body of Christ is on earth; hence Saul could persecute it.

Since the church is the body of Christ on earth, it ought to be manifested here. Although the head is in heaven and the body is on earth, they are yet one. That which is in heaven and that which is on earth are one. Hence, the persecution of the church is the persecution of the Lord;

persecuting the body is persecuting the head. The union is so perfect that it cannot be separated.

People may ask, "How could the body of Christ have been on earth during Paul's time? During the two thousand years from his time to the present, multitudes have been saved and added to the body of Christ. How, then, could the church be the body of Christ at such an early period?" J. B. Stoney, a very spiritual brother and greatly used by God in the last century, had a very good illustration. He said that the church is like a little bird. When it first breaks through its egg shell, it is called a bird, though its feathers have yet to be filled out. Later on, when it becomes full-grown, it is still called a bird. It is not denied the name of a bird when its feathers are not yet full. The feathers grow slowly from within; they are not stuck on from outside. All the growth comes from within until gradually the little bird becomes fully grown. And this is also the way the church exists on earth. Although at Paul's time it was just beginning, it nonetheless was the body of Christ. As of today, it has grown a great deal, but nothing foreign is to be added to it. All growth is from within.

Though the number of the saved in the church today is still far from complete, yet the church is perfect within. What is within it needs to be fully developed, that is, Christ must be manifested from within. Therefore, the church of today as well as the church of yesterday and the church of tomorrow is the body of Christ. God does not save people and add them to the church outwardly; rather, the body of Christ grows continuously from within, out of the head.

The church is none other than that which comes out of

Christ. It comes out of the head who is in heaven, but it dwells today on earth. It is a body. Like a little bird, it needs to grow until it is fully matured. The church, then, is one thing from beginning to end.

The Bible shows us that the basis of the church is the body of Christ. All that is not founded on the body of Christ is not the church. The Word of God recognizes only one church—the body of Christ. No matter for what reason or how scriptural, if something is not based on the body of Christ, it cannot be recognized as a church. When the influence of Protestantism was at its height in Europe, besides the national churches, many dissenting groups and many denominations sprang up. During that period, man-established churches sprouted like spring bamboo shoots after a fresh rain. They escaped from the bondage of the Roman Catholic Church and fled to the liberty of the Protestant churches. They fancied they had the freedom to establish churches. But were the churches they established founded on the principle of the body?

It is imperative that we see with accuracy before God what the church is. The church is the body of Christ. Anything that is smaller than the body of Christ cannot be used as the basis of a church. For example, we brethren in Shanghai have a church because we have learned to stand on the ground of the body and receive all members of the body of Christ for fellowship. We have only one condition for receiving brothers and sisters in the church here, and that is, that they belong to the body of Christ, that they are in the body. This alone justifies our being a church.

Once there is a church here in Shanghai, suppose the day comes when some of the brethren disagree with certain doctrines or feel that some truths held by the church are faulty. Do they have the right to set up another church? No, for they have no ground for it. The basis of the church is the body of Christ. To found a church in order to maintain a truth is not sufficient justification. If the church in Shanghai is not the body of Christ, then those brethren may establish a church. But if it is, then they have to continue their fellowship there. They are not free to set up another church.

Suppose some other brothers declare that they are not so much concerned with the doctrines of the Bible and their interpretation as with supplying spiritual food to those who gather. Can they form a church on the basis of this excellent motive to supply spiritual food to God's children? No, other societies may be set up at will but not a church. They may organize a Christian endeavor, a Sunday school, or a holy club, but they cannot institute a church Supplying spiritual food is not sufficient ground for forming a church. On one ground only may a church be established, and that is, it must include all of God's children. To put it another way, the church must take the body of Christ as its unit. If other people fail to gather together on the basis of that unit, the responsibility is theirs; but a church cannot have any condition other than belonging to the body. The body is, therefore, the one and only condition. The church must be as comprehensive as the body; it may not be smaller than the body. All who belong to Christ are included in the church. No one who is in the body of Christ may be rejected.

According to the Bible, the church of Christ is the body of Christ, and the body of Christ is the church of Christ. Not even a doctrine can be used as justification for founding a church. Holiness is important, for without holiness no one can see God. Faith is very necessary, for by faith we are justified. However, neither holiness nor faith may serve as the reason for establishing a church, for the church is the body of Christ. It is not the gathering of those who believe in the doctrine of holiness, nor is it an assembly of those who advocate justification by faith.

Certainly, nationality cannot be the ground of the church, such as the Lutheran Church in Germany or the Anglican Church in England. After God revealed to Martin Luther the truth of justification by faith, he was instrumental in spreading the Protestant movement. But this did not give him or his followers the right to establish a national church. If there are but ten Christians today standing on the ground of the body of Christ, they have the right to form a church. But Germany with her twenty million Christians cannot organize a church. Just because she has so many people is not sufficient cause for the establishment of a national church.

The ground of the church, therefore, is the body of Christ in a locality. It is not based on doctrine or nation, or on spiritual food or Biblical interpretation. Wherever we go, we must be clear of this one position: that the church is the body of Christ. If a local church is formed on this basis, it is not sectarian.

If some brothers and sisters hold different views and interpretations from you and therefore insist on setting up a separate meeting, their ground is wrong. Since yours is the body of Christ, you have the right ground. They have no ground, for theirs is based on views and interpretation. Of all the so-called churches in the world, only those which stand for the body of Christ are churches. The rest do not have sufficient basis to be considered a church.

If God's children clearly see that the body is the only ground of the church, they will not divide into sects. It may be all right to have a church with only three or five persons, but it may not be all right to establish one with a hundred or a thousand people. We are convinced that the church has only one basis: to fully manifest the body of Christ. We do not gather on any position other than that of the body of Christ. I do hope believers may see that wherever a group in a locality exceeds or undercuts the body of Christ, that group cannot be recognized as a church. The group that exceeds the body of Christ is that which receives people who do not belong to the body; it brings in unbelievers. Such groups become a mixture and lose the status of a church. On the other hand, any group which undercuts the body of Christ is that which narrows its fellowship. It may be a holiness group or a seventh-day group or a baptist group. Such groups restrict the body of Christ more than it should be; they too do not have sufficient ground to be recognized as a church.

Church Unity in the Holy Spirit

"For as the body is one, and hath many members, and all the members of the body, being many, are one body; so also is Christ. For in one Spirit were we all baptized into one body, whether Jews or Greeks, whether bond or free; and were all made to drink of one Spirit" (1 Cor. 12:12–13).

To say that the church comes out of Christ touches upon the matter of the source of the church. All Christians have new life. The one life of Christ has been multiplied into tens of thousands, and thousands of thousands of Christians. Chapter 12 of John shows us how a grain of wheat falls into the ground, dies, and bears many grains. All the

199

grains partake of the life of the first grain. One grain becomes many grains, and the many all come from the one grain.

We have seen how one grain can become many grains, but how can many grains again become one? Scripture shows us that the formation of the body of Christ is the work of the Holy Spirit. How does the Holy Spirit accomplish this work? He does it by baptizing many grains into one. From one Christ come the tens of thousands and thousands of thousands of Christians. These thousands of thousands of Christians are baptized into one body in one Spirit. Such is the basic teaching of 1 Corinthians 12:12–13. To use a different metaphor, we may say that all of us are like stones hewn out of the same rock and then cemented together into one whole by the Holy Spirit.

The body of Christ, then, has two basic principles: first, unless it comes out of Christ, it is not the body of Christ; second, unless there is the work of the Holy Spirit, it is not the body of Christ. We must be baptized in the Holy Spirit and be filled with the Holy Spirit so as to be joined into one. To say that the church begins at Pentecost is correct; to say it begins at the house of Cornelius is also correct; for both Jews and Gentiles have been baptized into one body. We first receive life from the Lord and this life is in the Holy Spirit in order to make us one body. Everyone who knows the Lord knows this body. Everyone who knows the Holy Spirit knows this body. If people walk according to the Holy Spirit, they are naturally aware of God's children being one body. The physical body has many members, but the head, through the nervous system, controls all the members. Likewise, the head of the church joins the many members together into one body through the Holy Spirit.

The Body the Basis of Fellowship

Let us reread 1 Corinthians 12:12: "For as the body is one, and hath many members, and all the members of the body, being many, are one body; so also is Christ."

The church comes out of Christ, and, through the operation of the Holy Spirit, becomes one body. All the members are fitted together and coordinated with one another in the Holy Spirit. Thus, the fellowship or communication of Christians, falls within the body. In other words, the basis for Christian fellowship is the body.

We are members one of another and we are one body. Naturally our fellowship is based on the body of Christ. There is no other relationship for fellowship except that we are all members of the body of Christ. We are neither all Jews nor all Greeks, all freemen nor all bondmen. We cannot base our fellowship on any of these relationships. Hence, the body is the one and only basis of our fellowship.

Any other communication cannot be recognized as Christian fellowship. Any communion, any gathering, or any group which is not conditioned by the body of Christ is not acceptable. Today there are a great number of so-called Christian fellowships, but their fellowships may not be based on being members one of another in the body. They may base their fellowship on a ritual (like immersion), a doctrine (like justification by faith), a form of government (like the episcopal), a person's name (such as Wesleyan), a certain system (like the congregational), or a certain movement (like the Pentecostal).

Thus many so-called Christian fellowships are without a right foundation before God. God's children ought to realize that the church is the body of Christ, and in that body a member is the smallest unit. The fellowship of all members is based on the body and nothing else. Such a basis for fellowship identifies a group as a Christian fellowship. Since you and I are members of the body of Christ we can fellowship together. Such fellowship of member with member is based on the oneness of the body. Because we share the same life in the body and are baptized in the same Holy Spirit, we are able to fellowship one with another. Our fellowship together should be maintained on no other basis.

Any fellowship other than that of the body is sectarian and divisive. If my arms and legs should organize a long limb club and hold fellowship on the basis of length, such fellowship would certainly be schismatic!

Let me repeat: fellowship which is not based on the body is not Christian fellowship. We cannot accept any fellowship that is different from the body. Nay, we must positively reject it. To keep our fellowship Christian means it should not be smaller than the body of Christ

The Ministry of the Body

For the body is not one member, but many. If the foot shall say, Because I am not the hand, I am not of the body; it is not therefore not of the body. And if the ear shall say, Because I am not the eye, I am not of the body; it is not therefore not of the body. If the whole body were an eye, where were the hearing? If the whole were hearing, where were the smelling? But now hath God set the members each one of them in the body, even as it pleased him. And if they were all one member, where were the body? . . . And God hath set some in the church, first apostles, secondly prophets, thirdly teachers, then miracles, then gifts of healings, helps, governments, divers kinds of tongues. Are all apostles? are all prophets? are all teachers?

202

are all workers of miracles? have all gifts of healings? do all
speak with tongues? do all interpret?

1 Cor. 12:14–19, 28–30

The Holy Spirit gives diverse gifts to the members of the
body of Christ according to the individual needs of the
body. The Lord's purpose in appointing the members to
different ministrations is to supply the needs of the body.
Thus He gives diversities of ministrations. He would never
make the body all eyes or ears or feet. The church needs
many different kinds of ministries in order to fulfill its
spiritual service. It needs the ministries of the Word, and it
needs the working of miracles. Both the ministry of the
Word and supernatural ministry are present in the body.

A church must have room for all the ministers (that is,
all the members) to serve the body. The church includes
all brothers and sisters, comely and uncomely. All have
their respective spiritual usefulness and all are engaged in
the Lord's service. The body should not have many useless
members. As everyone in the body is a member and each
member has his function, so every member ought to render
his service before God. This is how the church is manifested.

Upon reading Romans 12, Ephesians 4, and 1 Corinthians 12, we find that each member has his ministry and
that no matter how different the ministries may be, they
are all for the prosperity of the body. If you are a
Christian, you are a member of the body; as a member of
the body, you ought to contribute your part in the service
before God. We wish to reiterate the importance of
universal service. Everyone has his peculiar ministry. It is
absolutely necessary for everyone to serve. I do hope that
all God's children will come to that condition of serving
God.

If any system in a locality does not encourage all the members to serve but, rather, entrusts the affairs of the whole body to the eyes, that system undoubtedly is not of the body. How can you ask the eyes to do the work of the hands, to walk for the feet, to eat for the mouth, to smell for the nose or to touch for the fingers? If such a creature existed, made all of eyes, it would be a monster, not a body. Therefore, if you meet a group which adopts the system of letting one or two persons monopolize the management of the body affairs, thus discarding the services of the rest of the members, you know for sure that this is not the church. It is impossible for a body to grow in this way. Where have you seen a person who delegates the affairs of his whole body to one or two members—having the eyes do the hearing, smelling, talking, walking, working? You know such a condition is not the body of Christ, for something is drastically wrong.

We must see that in the church every member of the body has his ministry and therefore must serve. There is no monopoly of any kind; in service, one or two members cannot represent all the members. Any system which leaves no room for all the members to serve is decidedly not of the body. In the body, the eyes, the mouth, the feet, and the hands may all be busily engaged and there still be no conflict. If the mouth, the feet, the hands, or the nose are inactive, it means sickness has set in. When these different parts all function properly and coordinately in the body, then the body is seen. Likewise, if some serve and some do not, if some function as priests and some do not, or if the priesthood is left to one or a few persons, then it is only too clear that this is not the body. This principle, this way, must be understood by all the brothers and sisters.

The Body Life

For even as we have many members in one body, and all the members have not the same office: so we, who are many, are one body in Christ, and severally members one of another. And having gifts differing according to the grace that was given to us, whether prophecy, let us prophesy according to the proportion of our faith; or ministry, let us give ourselves to our ministry; or he that teacheth, to his teaching; or he that exhorteth, to his exhorting: he that giveth, let him do it with liberality; he that ruleth, with diligence; he that showeth mercy, with cheerfulness.

Rom. 12:4–8

Another thing to notice is that the grace which each one in the body receives is different. Due to this difference in grace, the gift each has from God is also different. First Corinthians 12 stresses the ministries of the Word and miraculous ministries, for such is its scope. But here in Romans 12, other than the ministries of the Word, there are the ministries of the church services. We may call these the works of the Levites. They are the ministries of giving, of ruling, of showing mercy, and of exhorting. We have both the ministries of the Word and the works of the Levites.

In 1 Corinthians 12 we have seen that the body should leave room for all the members to serve. Here in Romans 12 we further see that each gift, whether pertaining to the ministries of the Word or to the ministries of service, must be singly attended to. In other words, no one should interfere with another's business or step on another's toes. Just be faithful in the gift which is given to you. If it is prophesying, be so occupied in it that you will not be engaged in other things. If exhorting, exhort with all your

205

heart and do not be distracted toward other things. If ruling, be diligent in the church. Human nature is such that we delight to mind other people's business! But, as brethren, we should realize that every one of us must serve and serve faithfully in that which is given.

The body cannot afford to allow any member not to function. If the eyes do not see, the whole body is immobilized. The eyes should see, the feet should walk. Even the smallest of all gifts must not be buried. This is the principle of the one talent. It, too, must be used. When the body of Christ is serving as the church, every member's gift, whether large or small, five talents, two talents, or one talent, must be used. If people hide their one talent, the church will be seriously hurt.

First Corinthians 12 instructs us that one member should not usurp the place of another member; Romans 12 shows that no member should lose his place. We should neither occupy another's place nor lose our own place. Everyone should offer what he has and all should serve together. Thus is the church manifested.

Whether a church is prosperous or not depends less on the readiness of the persons with five talents as on the readiness of those with one talent. Through the centuries the difficulty has lain with those that have one talent, not with those that have five talents. The former tend to bury their talent in the ground. As a result, the church is weighed down by an incredible dead weight. Those with five talents have to bear the dead weight of the people with one talent. Wherever the people with one talent put in their one talent for trade, there is to be found the church.

It is worth noticing that the prosperity of a church depends less on the personal accomplishment of a few leaders as on their ability to inspire those with one talent to put that talent to use. The entire problem of the church today is with those people of one talent. The Lord has shown us that no one possesses more than five talents. In its perhaps twenty or so years of history, a church may only have one person with five talents, but she constantly has five persons with but one talent. However weak a child of God is, he still possesses at least one talent. Putting those five one-talents together is equal to one five-talents. If all the one-talent people would put theirs in, the church would have less need of the bigger gifts. The whole world could easily be conquered by sending forth all the one-talent people.

Let us clearly see, then, that the church must have more than the ministry of one person—no matter how capable that one person or how much he loads himself. To meet the church need, we should help all the brothers and sisters—all those with one talent—to join in the service of God. This is the way that we have especially seen during these years. All people with one talent must arise to serve the Lord. One person busy from morning till night cannot be considered the church. But if you are busy and you help all the one-talent people to be busy, then the church is in action: the church is serving, the church is preaching the gospel, the church is at work. It is the body in operation, not just a few members operating on behalf of the body.

Never think that wherever people are meeting together, there is the church. No, only the body of Christ is the church, and the body of Christ is sustained by the operation of all the members. The main problem lies with the people of one talent. Hence, it is our burden and expectation that wherever we work, we concentrate our effort not on the more talented but rather on the less gifted, on people with one talent. We hope that all the one-talents will be dug out of the earth. The napkin should be used for wiping away the perspiration, not for wrapping the silver (see Lk. 19:20)!

Let me tell you, when all those with one talent rise up to serve the Lord, then we will have the church in our midst. Today's predicament is due to the monopoly of service by the people with five talents and with two talents, thus leaving idle the people with one talent. We must show the one-talent people that, little as they have, they must serve and serve faithfully. This is called the body; this is body life. Let each one learn to serve God with what he has; let no one try to push his responsibility upon others. Then we shall see that the body of Christ with its body life is built on the people of one talent.

The Building of the Body

And he gave some to be apostles; and some, prophets; and some, evangelists; and some, pastors and teachers; for the perfecting of the saints, unto the work of ministering, unto the building up of the body of Christ: till we all attain unto the unity of the faith, and of the knowledge of the Son of God, unto a fullgrown man, unto the measure of the stature of the fulness of Christ.

Eph. 4:11–13

We find here five different kinds of people ministering to the building up of the body of Christ. These five kinds of people are somewhat different from those mentioned in Romans 12 and 1 Corinthians 12, for they all are ministers of God's Word. God gives these ministers of His Word to the church for the purpose of building up the body of Christ. New believers should seek before God to be such ministers. May many be brought into this ministry of the

Word, for it is especially effective in helping the body of Christ to grow into maturity.

On the other hand, if a so-called church never gives new believers opportunity to manifest whether they have this ministry of the Word, you may be sure it is only a church in name, not a church in reality. The body of Christ is not likely to be found wherever God-given gifts are blocked and no opportunity given for new believers to manifest their gifts.

The Testimony of the Body

The cup of blessing which we bless, is it not a communion of the blood of Christ? The bread which we break, is it not a communion of the body of Christ? seeing that we, who are many, are one bread, one body: for we all partake of the one bread.

1 Cor. 10;16–17

The church is the body of Christ. Her main task on earth is to manifest this body and the oneness of this body. She does not need to wait till she reaches heaven to manifest the oneness of the body. It is here on earth that she ought to manifest the oneness. Those who confine the manifestation of the oneness of the body to heaven are those who seek to maintain and strengthen sects and divisions.

"Seeing that we, who are many, are one bread, one body." The New Testament pays great attention to this matter of the breaking of bread. It is mentioned in Acts 20:7, "And upon the first day of the week, when we were gathered together to break bread," showing how God's children break bread in remembrance of the Lord every Lord's day. This act shows forth, on the one hand, how the

209

Lord's body was broken for us, and, on the other hand, how this body is one. The breaking speaks of our Lord's laying down His life on the cross for love of us, and the oneness tells of all God's children being one today.

The New Testament way is that we gather on each Lord's day and break bread. Every Lord's day we come to the Lord, acknowledging that He has been broken for us and that God's children are one. Do you see that this testifies, on the one hand, to the Lord's laying down His body for us, and, on the other hand, to the church being the body of Christ? The body is one, for we who are many are one bread. One bread, one body—to show forth oneness. All who know what the body of Christ is, give this testimony every Lord's day. We testify to the one bread and the one body. This is the testimony of the church as well as the work of the church.

If any group claims to have body fellowship rather than a restricted fellowship, and yet fails to gather before the bread as the early believers did, it is incomplete in its testimony. During the time of the apostles, they gathered every Lord's day to show forth the oneness of the body.

Some say they have the breaking of bread every week, but we would like to ask: is this breaking of bread the center of all the meetings or is it only an appendage? During the apostolic time, the churches gathered for the one purpose of breaking bread. The occasion at Troas was an exception, for there Paul spoke a long while. But due to his lengthy discourse, one young man fell from the upper chamber. Fortunately, he lived. That time, in order that Paul might preach, the breaking of bread was delayed. It was, nonetheless, exceptional. We must not purposely postpone the breaking of bread to the last minute in order to accommodate preaching. The question, therefore, is not simply whether or not there is the bread, but also how much standing it is given. This ought to be the center of all the gatherings of God's children.

Those who make preaching the main interest and thereby belittle the breaking of bread are quite ignorant of the truth of the body. The more we know the body of Christ, the better we understand how the breaking of bread manifests this truth. To break bread is indeed to remember the Lord's death, but it also manifests the oneness of the body. We, being many, are one body. We bring out the bread to show to the world that the church is one body. Consequently, let us do this on God's appointed day.

Finally, to gather up all these fragmentary thoughts about the body of Christ, it is our desire that you may see before God that the body of Christ is the basis for the fellowship of the church on earth. Beware of any fellowship that is other than the body. It must not be larger than the body—by bringing in unbelievers, nor should we make it smaller than the body—by excluding believers. We must maintain on earth the testimony of the one body. May God be gracious to us.

THE AUTHORITY OF THE CHURCH

We will now consider the matter of the authority of the church.

The Governing Principle of the Universe

Before God created the universe, He established a principle to govern it—the principle of authority. He Himself would be the highest authority and, at the same time, the source of all authority. Under Him would be several archangels, and under them would be many angels. On the earth would be other living creatures. That is how God arranged to govern the universe, and that is how it is. He upholds all things by the word of His power—the stars, the earth, and all the living creatures. He has established laws to regulate every living creature and every natural phenomenon. Therefore, authority is of paramount importance in the universe. If any living or non-living thing disobeys its law, it will bring chaos to the universe.

The History of Rebellion

1. THE REBELLION OF ANGELS—IN THE UNIVERSE

We know the former world fell through the self-exaltation of God's appointed archangel. Satan's rebellion was rebellion against authority. "And thou saidst in thy heart, I will ascend into heaven, I will exalt my throne above the stars of God . . . I will make myself like the Most High" (Is. 14:13–14). Satan desired to be equal with God: he wanted to exalt himself to be God; he was not content with exercising lordship over everything under God. He rebelled against God's authority, aiming at usurping it entirely. As a result, that bright morning star has become Satan; the angel of light has become the devil. This all happened before the creation of man.

2. THE REBELLION OF MAN—IN THE WORLD

After God created man, He put him in the Garden of Eden. In this present world, God has His own arrangement for the order of things and His own appointed authorities. Thus He created first the male and then the female. He made the husband before He built the wife. God's arrangement was that Eve should be subject to Adam and that man should be subject to God Himself. Later on, He also arranged for children to obey their parents, servants their masters, and the common people their kings and rulers.

But Satan enticed Eve in the garden. He did not try to tempt *man* to sin by getting him to overthrow God's appointed authority, but he sought out the *woman*. God's arrangement had been that the woman should listen to the man, but the temptation in the garden was to make man listen to the woman. God had appointed Adam to be head in the family, but this incident in the garden revealed that Eve was head. It was Eve who taught and decided and had an opinion. During those days, there was no one on earth but Adam and Eve—the rest of mankind had yet to be born. So we see here that God's order is for the woman to be subject to the man, the wife to the husband. But we also see that this order was almost immediately wrecked by Satan.

Though only two persons were involved in this wreckage, yet it was as if the whole world had rebelled. Not only was the authority between man and man broken, but the authority between man and God was also overthrown. Satan said, "In the day ye eat thereof . . . ye shall be as God" (Gen. 3:5). The insinuation was that God would not allow them to eat because He did not want them to be like Him. The result, therefore, was a twofold rebellion: man's rebellion against the authority which God had established among men, and man's rebellion against God's authority over him. In other words, God's delegated authority as well as God's direct authority were both violated. Instead of obeying God, man aspired to be like God. Thus the authority of God was subverted.

Eve should have been subject to Adam. She should have asked Adam. But instead of asking, she exercised her own mind and made her own decision. Consequently, Eve sinned first. Please remember: independent thinking is the harbinger of sin. If man does not learn to know God's mind or seek instruction from God's delegated authority, if he depends on his own independent thought—thinking this is good, it tastes fine, it feels good, I will gain wisdom by eating it—then he will not only have rebelled against God but also will have rebelled against God's established authority on earth. That is why the sin of the Garden of

Eden was a double subversion of the delegated as well as the direct authority of God.

The story of the Garden of Eden is really a duplicate of what Satan had done earlier. Satan had himself aspired to be equal with God, and then he tempted man to also exalt himself to be God. In the first paradise, the brilliant cherub conceived the idea of rebellion; in the second garden of pleasure, man rebelled. Ever since then, man has been going the way of rebellion. Hence, Romans 5 tells us that "through one trespass the judgment came unto all men to condemnation . . . For . . . through the one man's disobedience the many were made sinners" (vv. 18-19). Remember, in God's sight, what happened in the Garden of Eden was not only a matter of trespass but also one of disobedience. There was rebellion in the garden as well as sin. By the rebellion of one man, sin entered into the world. Thereafter, a life of rebellion became the principle of man.

After the flood, God ordained that certain men should be over their fellowmen. Thus the age of government was ushered in. From Adam to the flood, there were only families; but after the flood, government began. Government was instituted sixteen hundred fifty-six years after creation. As soon as the flood was over, we may see that the authority to rule was extended from the family to the government. "Whoso sheddeth man's blood, by man shall his blood be shed" (Gen. 9:6). This marked the beginning of government.

Following the flood, Ham rebelled against his father's authority (see Gen. 9:20-27). After that, the nations that God established joined to build the tower of Babel. Though there was no rebellion within their own ranks, yet these nations united together in rebellion against God. In the Garden of Eden, the rebellion was of one person or a family, but by the time of the tower of Babel, the rebellion was of nations. The people of the then existing world conspired to build a tower whose top might reach into heaven. They desired to go higher and higher until they could stand with God. Instead of using the stones God gave, they made bricks, trying to imitate God's work. They aspired to be equal with God.

3. THE REBELLION OF THE ISRAELITES

As a result, God chose Abraham who not only was the father of faith, but who also represented obedience. God chose him during those days of general confusion and rebellion of the nations. God longed for those who would stand in the place of obedience in the midst of rebellion.

Not only was Abraham himself obedient, so also was his wife. Abraham and Sarah both obeyed God, and Sarah was obedient to Abraham. Sarah accepted God's delegated authority (Abraham) as well as God's direct authority. They both were obedient to God; and between them, that is, between husband and wife, there was also obedience. Because they maintained the principle of God's authority on earth, the people of God were to come from them. God's people were chosen on the basis of God's authority.

God promised Abraham that, though his descendants would be slaves in Egypt, yet in the fourth generation they would come out. This was fulfilled in the story of the exodus, which tells how Moses led out the people of Israel. God first apprehended Moses, and caused him to know authority and learn obedience; then He used him to bring out the Israelites. Here too, among the Israelites, God set up His direct authority. During the exodus, God was present with the people in the pillar of cloud and of fire. He gave them the commandments, signifying His direct authority. He also chose Moses and Aaron, signifying His representative authority. Thus Moses and Aaron became God's delegated authorities among the people of Israel.

As God would not allow anyone to commit an offense against Himself, so He would not allow anyone to commit an offense against His servants. As He did not permit the people to sin against Him, so He would not permit them to sin against His prophet and His priest, for He had established His authority among the people of Israel. Many times the Israelites were judged and punished because they violated God's authority. For this very reason, many of them were barred from entering Canaan.

After the Israelites did enter the land of Canaan, they were again disobedient to God. Their disobedience was so serious as to cause them to want someone from among them to be their king. They were not pleased with God's rule over them; they preferred to imitate the nations around them. God told Samuel that, "they have not rejected thee, but they have rejected me, that I should not be king over them" (1 Sam. 8:7). Saul was the first king chosen, and after him, David. God appointed David to be the authority. David prepared materials for building the temple. The temple signified that God and His people dwelt together. It was Solomon who built that house.

Even before Solomon passed away, the people of Israel began to worship idols. Thus it was that God rejected the kingdoms of Israel and of Judah. Although He allowed them to continue for some years and have more kings, he did it only because of His promise to David. You can see

218

here that no sin offends God more than the sin of idolatry, for idolatry stands in the place of worship to God. After idolatry came in, Israel's subsequent history was full of rebellion.

The Principle of Obedience

Not until the Lord Jesus was born did God find His chosen One. The Lord Himself told us, "The Son can do nothing of himself, but what he seeth the Father doing; for what things soever he doeth, these the Son also doeth in like manner" (John 5:19); "I do nothing of myself, but as the Father taught me, I speak these things" (John 8:28); "I seek not mine own will, but the will of him that sent me" (John 5:30). Here we find a Man who yielded absolutely to God's authority.

The Lord Jesus was Himself God and yet He did not count being on an equality with God a thing to be grasped; rather, He submitted Himself wholly to the authority of God. After He died on the cross, God raised Him from among the dead and highly exalted Him. He was made Lord and Christ, and was given "the name which is above every name, that in the name of Jesus every knee should bow, of things in heaven and things on earth and things under the earth, and that every tongue should confess that Jesus Christ is Lord, to the glory of God the Father" (see Phil. 2:5–11).

After the ascension of the Lord, His church was formed. He did not establish His church as an organization or institution according to the expectation of men. This Lord who arose from the dead and ascended on high is to be the head of the church, and the whole church is to be His

219

body. In other words, as He lived a life of obedience on earth, so He wishes His church to once again manifest an obedient life today.

In the Bible, the gospel itself is also a command. We are exhorted not only to believe the gospel, but also to obey. The Holy Spirit is given to those who obey God, that is, to those who obey the word which is preached. Remember, obedience is involved in the very acceptance of the Lord Jesus. It is God's command that men everywhere should believe. Believing, therefore, is obeying. From the very start, those who are in the church ought to learn how to obey the Lord, how to obey God's authority.

During the many centuries of human history, the world has always been rebellious. A basic principle of the world is the overthrow of God's authority, direct or delegated. But when the church, the body of Christ, was established on earth, her basic principle was that of obedience. What God originally designed for the world is now strictly required of the church. Today God seriously demands that in the church the women be subject to the men. How hard that would be for the world! Ask any woman in the world if she is willing to be subject to man. Her answer would be no, that she has not the slightest inclination in that direction. But in the church, God asks the woman to obey the man and the wife to be subject to her husband.

In the highly spiritual epistles of Ephesians and Colossians, the Lord charges wives to be subject to their husbands, children to obey their parents, and servants to be obedient to their masters. These are not words for the world but words for the church.

Both epistles rank among the greatest. They show us how we were once sons of disobedience because our life principle was not different from that of other worldly people—the principle of disobedience. But now God has given us a command: wives be subject to husbands, children obey parents, servants be obedient to masters. This is so different from the entire world. Thus we see that the basic principle of the church today is obedience.

Later on, we find such clear words in Romans as, "Let every soul be in subjection to the higher powers: for there is no power but of God; and the powers that be are ordained of God" (13:1). All powers are ordained of God, therefore we must be in subjection to authorities and rulers. "Render to all their dues; tribute to whom tribute is due; custom to whom custom; fear to whom fear; honor to whom honor" (13:7). There is no book which presents salvation so clearly as the book of Romans. But from the twelfth chapter, beginning with consecration, up to the fourteenth chapter, we are told that we must be in subjection not only in the body (the church) but also in the world. Men must be in subjection to all higher powers.

The Authority Upheld

The church is a corporate body having the special characteristic that its members, as long as they live in this world, live in obedience. We take obedience as our principle of daily life.

The church today needs to be brought to the place where she can declare that what God did not obtain at the time of Adam, He now has obtained in her. That which God failed to get from the nation of Israel is today found in the church. What the world—the men of every tribe and tongue and people and nation—does not have, the church does have. In other words, on this huge earth there is at least one group of people which upholds the authority of God. Though the people in this wide, wide world are rebellious, the church is the one body that is obedient to authority. She should be able to lift up her head and say, "Lord, what You did not get from Satan and his rebellious followers, You now have in the church."

Thus, unto the principalities and the powers in the heavenly places, God's authority is now made manifest through the church. The church today is not only on the earth to preach the gospel and to build herself up but also to manifest the authority of God. Everywhere else God's authority is rejected, but here in the church His authority is upheld. People in the world do not seek the will of God, but the church is here seeking His will. In other words, the church is an obedient body. If you are unsaved and therefore not in the church, you are excepted; otherwise, once you come into the church, you must before God uphold this one basic principle of enabling God's authority to be accomplished in the church. God's will cannot get through anywhere in the world, but His will should be able to prevail in the church. You and I must uphold God's authority in the church.

For this reason, the brothers and sisters in the church must all learn to be obedient. Please bear in mind that no sin is more serious than that of disobedience, for it contradicts the very reason for the church's existence. What mattered with the Lord Jesus on earth was not whether He lived well but whether He was obedient. As a matter of fact, if the Son had done anything on His own, it could only have been good. But He insisted that He could do nothing by Himself, for He did not come to do His own will but to do the will of the Father who sent Him. Remember, there is one authority in the universe that must be upheld, and the Lord did uphold it. Today, may the church do the same.

What God earlier failed to obtain in different dispensations He will obtain in the church. What He has failed to get elsewhere, He will now have in the church. Hence the church is the only place where you can learn the lesson of obedience. In the church, we speak not only of good or bad, right or wrong, but, even more, of obedience. We need to see that there is no testimony more important today than the testimony of obedience. Because the whole universe has fallen into rebellion, God is not able to find any place at all except in the church where men will accept His authority. For this reason, God's children must learn to obey in the church.

Obedience is the life of the church. It is her very nature and, therefore, her basic principle. She exists for the purpose of upholding obedience. She is the precise opposite of the condition of the surrounding nations. While the nations of the earth take counsel together against God and against His anointed, saying, "Let us break their bonds asunder, and cast away their cords from us" (Ps. 2:3), while they struggle to be free of the law of the Son of God, the church declares with joy, "I most gladly put myself under His bonds and His cords in order to learn obedience." This is the church. She becomes not only a body which obeys the direct authority of God but also an organ for the testimony of obedience. She upholds on earth God's indirect, delegated authority as well as God's direct authority.

The Authority of the Church

In the Bible much is said about obedience. For our present purpose we will view obedience in four sections.

1. THE LAW OF THE BODY

The church is the body of Christ. Within the body is an inherent law. Every member has his use, and every member is governed by a strange and mysterious law of function. It is imperative for the members to learn how to be subject to the law of the body. If any member should act independently, out of his own idea, it betrays a sickness. The characteristic of the body is oneness. When that oneness is wrecked, the body most surely is sick.

For this reason, no child of God should violate the law of the body of Christ and act independently. Independent actions always speak of rebellion. Rebellion is expressed by independent action. To act independently is to not be in subjection to the authority of the head, to the principle of oneness which God has ordained for the body, or to the law of oneness prescribed in the Bible. Independent action is both a matter of disobedience to the Lord and of insubjection to the body.

The Lord baptized all His children into one body in the Holy Spirit. This inward unity is exceedingly intimate. If one member rejoices, the whole body is joyful; if one member suffers, the whole body suffers. Such an inward relationship is beyond understanding. Many times a brother has come to me, wondering why his heart is so troubled today without reason, or why he has felt so happy the last two days? I do not know how to explain. But often the reason cannot be found in yourself, for you have no reason to be especially happy or to be unusually sad. There are many functions in the body which are beyond explanation. When we stand before the Lord in the future, then we shall know why we were so strangely strengthened or so strangely weakened certain days or why we had special feelings at other times. Do remember, other members may influence us, even as we may influence them. Although we are ignorant of how such influences operate, we do know that our oneness is a fact. We are not clear today of the how, but through experience we know that we are one and that the various members in the body do affect one another.

There is a law among us which we all must obey: what the whole body sees before God, I must see; what the whole body rejects or accepts before God, I must reject or accept. As a member of the body, I cannot function independently. The body has its law, and oneness is its authority. I cannot act according to my own wish; if I do, I am rebellious and disobedient to authority. The body is authority; the body is representative of the authority of Christ. If I leave the body and engage in independent action, I am a rebel.

Let me use cancer as an illustration. Of all the sicknesses, cancer is one of the most terrible. It is much more troublesome than tuberculosis. Normally, the cells of the human body multiply by division: one cell divides into two, two into four, four into eight, and so forth. Every cell has the power of growth, and there is a law within which governs its growth.

For example: Today I carelessly cut my hand. The cells around the wound start to multiply by division until the wound is closed. Who tells these cells to grow? How do they grow? We do not know. But we do understand that it is right for them to grow, because I have a wound. We also reckon it right for them to cease growing after the wound is closed. So here is a law which every cell knows. It knows how to obey the law of growth or the law of cessation of growth in the body.

Now remember that the law of the entire spiritual body is the authority of God—which we must learn to obey. But if we disobey, let me tell you, something terrible happens. If my hand is cut and the cells around the wound start to grow, fine; but if they continue to grow after the wound has closed, what then? It has become a cancer. A cancer is cells which depart from the law ordained for all the cells of the body, which grow when there is no need in the body, and grow independently and unceasingly.

Every cell must be under control. Yet here is a cell which grows, irrespective of the law of the cells. It simply keeps on growing, disregarding all the other cells. Such a cell is malignant. Its growth affects the whole body. The cancer cell draws upon the other cells of the body to help it grow, instead of its helping the body grow. All the cells in the body ought to grow for the welfare of the body, but now they are adversely affected by the cancer cell and become its accomplices. The cancer cell has departed from the law of the body and has been changed into an abnormal cell.

So if a person is disobedient to authority and to the law of the body and acts in accordance with his own ideas, rather than in accordance with the principle of oneness, he becomes a cancer. Whoever gets in touch with him will be used to develop him and not the body. He will absorb everything around him to expand himself instead of increasing the body. He acts on a principle different than that of the body.

The body of Christ is living. We may claim that there is nothing more living, more one, more full of life than the body. If, before you trusted the Lord, you were accustomed to acting independently, you need to realize that after you believe, you become a cell in the body; you are a member

226

of the body. Every cell is controlled by the law of the body. You must follow the law of the body, not your own wish. If you insist on following your own idea, you become a cancer in the body. This is something harmful, not helpful, to the body.

We are fearful of those who act independently, those who reject the control of the body and follow their own whims, who do not learn to obey the authority of the head in the body. After we have believed in the Lord, the first spiritual principle we should remember is that the body is God's ordained authority on earth. The body is an authority. God's law is in the body and I must not violate it. I cannot follow my own will I dare not do anything by myself, for if I do, I become as an uncontrollable malignant cell in the body, working for myself and destroying the oneness of the body. I will be a cancer, unable to coordinate with others, totally independent, detrimental to the body. Let us therefore learn to accept the judgment of the body and learn to follow the movement of life in the entire body.

The longer you are before the Lord as a Christian, the more you see that the oneness of the body is a fact. You see that it is a tremendously serious fact and that therefore you must learn not to corrupt it. If you break it, you are lawless, disobedient, and rebellious, and the authority of God is not upon you. As we no doubt realize, authority must be upon each cell, for the cells of the body must work together, not independently. This is most marvelous. How appropriate it is that Scripture uses the body as an illustration of the church.

2. THE PRINCIPLE OF TWO OR THREE

There is another principle in the Bible which we must obey: the principle of two or three.

And if thy brother sin against thee, go, show him his fault between thee and him alone: if he hear thee, thou hast gained thy brother. But if he hear thee not, take with thee one or two more, that at the mouth of two witnesses or three every word may be established. And if he refuse to hear them, tell it unto the church, and if he refuse to hear the church also, let him be unto thee as the Gentile and the publican. Verily I say unto you, What things soever ye shall bind on earth shall be bound in heaven; and what things soever ye shall loose on earth shall be loosed in heaven. Again I say unto you, that if two of you shall agree on earth as touching anything that they shall ask, it shall be done for them of my Father who is in heaven. For where two or three are gathered together in my name, there am I in the midst of them.

Matt. 18:15–20

The Lord Jesus tells us that if two or three gather together in His name or unto His name in one accord, as harmonious as music, He is in the midst of them. Whatever thing they ask shall be done for them. This, indeed, is a great promise given to us by the Lord. If two or three agree perfectly and doubt not, the Lord promises to answer their prayer.

The Lord also tells me what I should do if I sin against a brother and he comes to enlighten me as to how I have been wrong, and yet I still feel I was right. The Lord tells me I should learn to listen to my brother. If I am a person who before the Lord has learned to receive, then I will immediately sense my sin when my brother comes to talk to me. Why? Because this too is a body principle—one person may represent the body. In spite of how right I feel, if I am a meek and lowly person before God, I will acknowledge that my brother has more experience and is more deeply instructed before the Lord. He sees my fault and now comes to correct me.

Let me say that one person can be authority. You do not need to wait for more. The person next to you may be that authority; he may represent the body, for one person can represent the entire church. I should see that my action was wrong, for that person has given evidence of it. I do not mean there has to be evidence before you accept it. What I say is that you need to be sensitive before God. Thus, many times it will be unnecessary for you to be told by two or three people or by the whole church. In the realm of spiritual reality, we ought to be able to see and touch a matter when we are told by one person. That one person is already the body, for he represents the body.

Sometimes, there is need for the witness of two and three. If a brother comes to help me and I still cannot see, he will go and get another brother or two. The other brother or brothers are known for their whole-hearted love toward the Lord. They are people of spiritual stature and mature in the Lord's service. These two or three inform me that, so far as they understand, I am in the wrong. At that time, I should remember what the Lord has said, "For where two or three are gathered together in My name, there am I in the midst of them."

If those two or three agree in dealing with a matter, their prayer will be heard by the Lord. If the Lord hears them, can I reject their dealing with me? If the Lord accepts their judgment, who am I to reject it? Since the Lord accepts what they do with one accord as right, how can I say it is not right? I should listen to them right away. Knowing that what they bind on earth shall be bound in heaven and what they loose on earth shall be loosed in heaven, I cannot but follow the decision of heaven.

Two or three persons become authority. This, of course, does not mean that any two or three brothers can be randomly invited or can speak carelessly. These brothers must be those who have authority before the Lord, who are godly and obedient. If they are in agreement and say you are wrong, I suggest that you be in subjection and acknowledge your fault—even if you feel otherwise. You do not need to wait till the whole church advises you. If you are highly sensitive, the testimony of one person will be enough. If you are less sensitive, two or three persons speaking to you ought to be sufficient to bring you to your senses. When the godly two or three agree, your attitude before God should be submissive, not arrogant.

3. SUBJECTION TO CHURCH AUTHORITY

Matthew 18 further shows us that if two or three brothers fail to convince you, they should bring the matter to the church. The whole church then should deliberate before God. If the decision still is against you, what will you say then? Will you say, "Though the body judges me to be wrong, the head reckons me right; though my parents forsake me, the Lord keeps me; though my brethren reject me, the Lord receives me. I will bear the cross here"? No, such an attitude would show that you are outside the church. How can you consider yourself persecuted and ill-treated, suffering at the hands of your brethren? My advice to you is to humble yourself and say, "Whatever the church says is right, for there can be no further judgment. If all the brothers and sisters say I am wrong, I am wrong, in spite of my own feeling." We need to learn how to be in subjection to the authority of the church.

There is the authority of God in the church. Do not be so hardened as to refute the decision of the brotherhood. A proud person has no place in the church, for he knows neither obedience nor the church. Let us learn to be gentle, humble, and submissive. The church has authority before God. What the church rejects, God rejects.

Every child of God needs to learn obedience in the church. It may be one person, two or three persons, or sometimes even the whole local assembly, but each of these are representative of the church. We must learn to be gentle and tender before God. Do not be hard and arrogant. God's children stand by the principle of obedience.

4. REPRESENTATIVE AUTHORITY IN THE CHURCH

Besides those already mentioned, the Bible indicates there are others who represent authority in the church.

THE RESPONSIBLE BROTHERS—THE ELDERS

The Bible shows us that those who are responsible brothers before the Lord, those who are overseers or elders, represent God's authority in the church in a special way. The other brethren should learn how to stand in a position of subjection to them before God. The work of those whom God appoints to authority in the church is to oversee all the affairs of the church. Hence, the brethren should learn to accept their decisions and to be in subjection to them.

God's children should seek everywhere for commands to follow and for opportunities to obey. They must not seek only for work to do. I often feel that many young people do not have much usefulness. Why? Because, though they may have many works to do, they just cannot obey. Many are disobedient. If you ask someone how long he has been working, he may answer that he has worked for the Lord ten years and has done many things. If you ask him to whom he has been in subjection throughout his lifetime, he may have nothing to say. Perhaps he never has subjected himself to anyone. Nevertheless, the basic principle of life in the church is obedience.

Everyone among us ought to learn obedience. It is most pitiful if a person never in his life learns subjection. We must be obedient to the church, God's ordained authority on earth, as well as to God Himself. We must also obey the authority which God establishes in the church—the responsible brothers.

ELDERLY AND ADVANCED BRETHREN

"Now I beseech you, brethren (ye know the house of Stephanas, that it is the firstfruits of Achaia, and that they have set themselves to minister unto the saints), that ye also be in subjection unto such, and to every one that helpeth in the work and laboreth" (1 Cor. 16:15–16). Those of the house of Stephanas had no thought but to serve the saints in the church at Corinth. Paul exhorted the saints to be in subjection to them. Whoever is appointed of God to be authority in the church is to be obeyed. The Corinthian believers must be in subjection to the house of Stephanas and to those who labored with Stephanas. We too must respect those who are older than us, who have been in Christ longer as firstfruits and who have set themselves to minister to us. Never think that you can reject them. No, they should be obeyed.

"Likewise, ye younger, be subject unto the elder" (1 Pet. 5:5). The preceding verses show us that those referred to in this passage are those who came to know the Lord earlier and who serve as elders of the church. The younger should be in subjection to the elder, for they make themselves examples to the flock (v. 3), and they exercise oversight according to the will of God (v. 2). Those elder brothers who especially represent the Lord in the church ought to receive special obedience from the rest of the believers.

"Let the elders that rule well be counted worthy of double honor, especially those who labor in the word and in teaching" (1 Tim. 5:17). Double honor should be paid to the elders who rule well in the church; no one may speak casually about them. We should honor the elders, particularly those who also labor in teaching. Some elders have the ministry of the Word; some do not. But all should be honored.

I wish to add a word of reminder here: many brothers and sisters have a basic misunderstanding about obedience—they choose the object of their obedience. They think that those whom they obey should be perfect. But, remember, the Lord never made such a rule. Obedience is not toward the perfect but only to the authority of the Lord in a person. If you want to choose whom you obey, you will always be able to find some faults. Frankly, even if Paul or Peter were in your midst, you would still easily pick out faults.

If you desire to find excuses, there will be many reasons why you will have no trouble in doing so. Here is an elder who only knows how to rule but has no ministry of the Word. You may conclude that he is not worthy of your respect because you can preach better than he does. Nevertheless, God's Word states clearly, "Let the elders that rule well be counted worthy of double honor, especially those who labor in the word and in teaching." The question of choice does not enter into this area. Many want to make their own choice in order to cover up their lawlessness and rebellion. This is folly. You should be in subjection to those who are elderly and more advanced, and not criticize them.

LEADERS

"Obey them that have the rule over you, and submit to them: for they watch in behalf of your souls, as they that shall give account" (Heb. 13:17). The Word of God is quite clear that we must obey those who watch over our own souls. There is no such thing as our choosing whom to obey. It would create great difficulty if we were to listen to one brother and not to another. Do remember that there is nothing unusual in hearkening to what a brother says. We all must learn to obey those who are ahead of us as well as those who are above us. We must learn to obey those who lead us as well as those who are especially gifted and greatly used of the Lord. We should always seek to find out who those ahead of us are.

Suppose you go to a place where three or four brothers are gathered together. Your first question should be, "Whom should I obey?" You ought to be in subjection to those ahead of you. Within only two or three hours you will naturally find out whom God is using to lead you. To that person you give your obedience. The characteristic of a Christian is obedience, not work. A mark of a Christian is his ability to recognize those who lead him. I often feel how very beautiful, spiritually beautiful, it is if, in a locality where there are only five or so brothers gathering together, each one stands in his place.

Why must we obey those who lead us? "For they watch in behalf of your souls, as they that shall give account; that they may do this with joy, and not with grief: for this were unprofitable for you." Whoever is ahead of you and watches over your soul in order to give an account before God, that is the person to whom you must render your submission.

LABORERS AMONG US

"But we beseech you, brethren, to know them that labor among you, and are over you in the Lord, and admonish you; and to esteem them exceeding highly in love for their work's sake" (1 Thes. 5:12–13). Some are used of the Lord to lead, to admonish, and to rule over you. To them you should give respect and honor. To them you should give obedience. If a Christian can find no one on earth to obey, he will be the strangest person in the world. A Christian ought to be able to see people everywhere who are ahead of him, who carry more spiritual weight, and who watch over his soul. It is to them that he should subject himself.

This being the case, the church must uphold this one principle—a principle which God cannot find in Satan, in the world, or in the universe. This principle is obedience. It is the basic lesson of the church. What the world rejects, the church gains. The basic principle of the church is obedience.

We have seen how the oneness of the body is authority. We have also seen how one person, two or three persons, or the local assembly may represent the body of Christ. Lastly, we have seen that the elders in the Lord, those who lead, also represent the body of Christ. These all are God's ordained authorities in our midst. We must obey them, respect them, learn from them, and listen to their words. Thus shall the name of the Lord and His Word be in our midst. Thus shall we be Philadelphia.

TITLES YOU
WILL WANT TO HAVE

By Watchman Nee

Basic Lesson Series
Volume 1 – A Living Sacrifice
Volume 2 – The Good Confession
Volume 3 – Assembling Together
Volume 4- Not I, But Christ
Volume 5 – Do All to the Glory of God
Volume 6 – Love One Another

The Church and the Work
Volume 1 – Assembly Life
Volume 2 – Rethinking the Work
Volume 3 – Church Affairs
Revive Thy Work
The Word of the Cross
The Communion of the Holy Spirit
The Finest of the Wheat – Volume 1
The Finest of the Wheat – Volume 2
Take Heed
Worship God
Interpreting Matthew
The Character of God's Workman
Gleanings in the Fields of Boaz
The Spirit of the Gospel
The life That Wins
From Glory to Glory
The Spirit of Judgment
From Faith to Faith
Back to the Cross
The Lord My Portion
Aids to "Revelation"
Grace for Grace
The Better Covenant
A Balanced Christian Life
The Mystery of Creation

The Messenger of the Cross
Full of Grace and Truth – Volume 1
Full of Grace and Truth – Volume 2
The Spirit of Wisdom and Revelation
Whom Shall I Send?
The Testimony of God
The Salvation of the Soul
The King and the Kingdom of Heaven
The Body of Christ: A Reality
Let Us Pray
God's Plan and the Overcomers
The Glory of His Life
"Come, Lord Jesus"
Practical Issues of This Life
Gospel Dialogue
God's Work
Ye Search the Scriptures
The Prayer Ministry of the Church
Christ the Sum of All Spiritual Things
Spiritual Knowledge
The Latent Power of the Soul
The Ministry of God's Word
Spiritual Reality or Obsession
The Spiritual Man
The Release of The Spirit
Spiritual Authority

By Stephen Kaung

Discipled to Christ
The Splendor of His Ways
Seeing the Lord's End in Job
The Songs of Degrees
Meditations on Fifteen Psalms

ORDER FROM:

Christian Fellowship Publishers, Inc.
11515 Allecingie Parkway
Richmond, Virginia 23235